**Modern Poetry in Tr**
Series Three, Numbe.

# Polyphony

Edited by David and Helen Constantine

MODERN POETRY IN TRANSLATION

Modern Poetry in Translation
Series Three, No. 13
© Modern Poetry in Translation 2010 and contributors
ISBN 978-0-9559064-5-9

Printed and bound in Great Britain by Short Run Press, Exeter

Submissions should be sent in hard copy, with return postage, to David
and Helen Constantine, *Modern Poetry in Translation*, The Queen's College,
Oxford, OX1 4AW. Unless agreed in advance, submissions by email will
not be accepted. Only very exceptionally will we consider work that has
already been published elsewhere. Translators are themselves responsible
for obtaining any necessary permissions. Since we do sometimes authorize
further publication on one or two very reputable websites of work that has
appeared in *MPT*, the permissions should cover that possibility.

Founding Editors: Ted Hughes and Daniel Weissbort

**Subscription Rates:** (including postage)

|  | UK | Overseas |
|---|---|---|
| Single Issue | £9.95 | £12.50 / US$ 21 |
| One year subscription (2 issues, surface mail) | £19.90 | £25.00 / US$ 42 |
| Two year subscription (4 issues, surface mail) | £36.00 | £46.00 / US$ 77 |

To subscribe please use the subscription form at the back of the magazine.
Discounts available.

To pay by credit card please visit www.mptmagazine.com

Modern Poetry in Translation is represented in the UK by
Central Books, 99 Wallis Road, London, E9 5LN

For orders: tel +44 (0) 845 458 9911 Fax +44 (0) 845 458 9912
or visit www.mptmagazine.com

Modern Poetry in Translation Limited. A Company Limited by Guarantee.
Registered in England and Wales, Number 5881603.
UK Registered Charity Number 1118223.

# Contents

# Editorial

This issue, like the last, drew much good work in under its title. For 'polyphony', many voices, is just as suggestive of the idea and the practice of translation as is 'transplanting'.

Voice is of the essence in poetry. We listen for and learn to love a poet's particular voice. In all the many voices that a poet may adopt, in all the personae (masks that the voice sounds through), still we pick up a tone and rhythm, an audible and palpable signature, that is unique. So there is distinctiveness, unmistakeable peculiarity in the whole polyphonic oeuvre of a poet's writing life. We speak of the moment of breakthrough, when the poet, having struggled among possibilities for a true identity, comes into his or her own voice. And that voice will be unique – and as various as the different poetic projects require it to be.

The translator doubles the foreign poet's uniqueness and multiplicity. The translator must have a voice. Translation is not a colourless medium through which the foreign writing passes straight and pure. Translation, even cleaving close, refracts and colours. These impurities (by which is not meant lexical and grammatical errors and arbitrary distortions of the text) should be welcomed, not regretted. They are the translator's own identity and tone. All translation, and especially the translation of poetry, is a struggle, a sort of contrapuntal contest, between two equally pressing demands: that of service, to the text; that of autonomy, for the making of an equivalent new poem. All the fun and anguish lies in that tension between service and self-assertion. The translator must have a voice and must assert it. Ideally, it should be as unique and multiple as that of the poet he or she translates, so serving the foreign poet in a voice recognizable as the translator's own.

Poems come alive when a reader reads them, they come off the page into a living voice. Every reader voices a poem distinctively. Readers are like the different singers of a song: the same words, the same tune – the rendition quite distinct. And of course, at different points in your life you will read the same poem differently. MacNeice was right to call the world 'incorrigibly plural'. Our life in it is polyphonic. We want a poetics (and a practice of translation) true to that.

When we redefined the 'modern' in *Modern Poetry in Translation* to mean any modern translation of any poetry however ancient, we greatly extended our world. We took down the frontier between us and the timeless dead. Every translator and every reader of a translation continues the lives of the dead. This issue of *MPT* is characteristically rich in that respect. To bring a dead writer's or singer's words across the Styx into the living here and now, that is an extension any human would be glad of.

David and Helen Constantine
August 2010

# The Next Issue of *MPT*

The next issue of *Modern Poetry in Translation* (Third Series, Number 15, spring 2011) will be called 'Poetry and the State'.

Poetry matters, and it matters that poetry should be translated and move freely across the frontiers of time and space. These are the premises on which we edit and poets and translators from all over the world contribute to *MPT*. But we want the next issue to *prove* a truth we hold to be self-evident: that poetry is necessary for a humane life. Some states encourage their poets, others ignore them, others imprison and murder them. We want to document – chiefly in translated poems, but also in statements and short essays – the varying but never easy relationship between poetry and the state. That does not mean we are only on the look-out for 'political' poems. Any lyric poem, insisting on the value of individual experience, lives in more or less uneasy dealings with the order and the ideology of the state. Does the state allow you the autonomy the poem demands? As always, we seek contributions from the present and the past, from near and far.

Submissions should be sent by 1 February 2011, please, in hard copy, with return postage, to The Editors, Modern Poetry in Translation, The Queen's College, Oxford, OX1 4AW. Unless agreed in advance, submissions by email will not be accepted. Only very exceptionally will we consider work that has already been published elsewhere. Translators are themselves responsible for obtaining any necessary permissions. Since we do sometimes authorize further publication on one or two very reputable websites of work that has appeared in *MPT*, the permissions should cover that possibility.

# Tony Baker
## 'Government by Unparliament': some drifts for catching about polyphony.

Between spring and early summer anyone walking near the sluggish stream that runs along the boundary to our village is likely to trigger a chorus of calls from the horny frogs that float there, half-submerged, peering out from amongst the duckweed. One frog will begin croaking and, in a few instants, it will have set off a host of others doing not quite exactly the same thing. What begins with a distinct, solitary voice rapidly turns into a trembling monotony that squats the air like the background noise of machinery on a factory floor. In that mass of noise the individual croakings become nearly indistinguishable.

In *Williams Mix*, the first piece John Cage invented for tape recorder, the 192-page graphic score indicates how the 600-odd discrete fragments of recorded sound should be spliced together and overlaid. The work took Cage nearly a year to assemble and prominently features, amongst multifarious other things, the clicks, croaks and whistlings of frogs. Each shard of sound lasts just long enough for the ear to begin to identify it. In Cage's mass of noise the voices of individual frogs become nearly distinguishable.

\*     \*     \*

One of my favourite tracks in recorded music is 'My Foolish Heart' from the set the Bill Evans trio played in 1961 at the Village Vanguard. LaFaro's melodic approach to the bass was so formative on Evans's piano-playing, and in particular on how he chose to voice the chords in his left hand that when LaFaro died a few days later in a car crash, Evans was musically orphaned. His voice was bound up with Lafaro's so completely that for months after his death Evans couldn't play.

Yet it's not just the extraordinary intimacy and intricacy of the way Evans and LaFaro lace their musical ideas together that's so striking about that recording. What sticks in the mind is how the microphones pick up the sounds of wineglasses and of knives and forks (?) from the listening public. The way the sound from the world beyond the trio leaks into their playing (the timbre of Motian's brushwork belongs to a palette that could easily include cutlery) and takes its place in the music as if by design, is polyphonic in a rich sense.

*       *       *

One time, short of a double-bassist for a gig, I suggested a possible replacement to another member of the band. He replied, 'don't ask him – he doesn't listen enough.'

*       *       *

The streetlights here go out well before midnight so when the sky's clear we enjoy a vista of stars that are invisible in town. When she was little, I tried to explain to my daughter that at one time it was thought that the turning of the stars made a heavenly music, that they were the parts of a perfectly tuned machine and that their twinklings were the notes of the universe. She said, 'you mean, like a piano'. I thought about this and it seemed quite a good comparison. I could see how the interplay between a piano's hammers and strings and the seemingly independent elements of the mechanism that brought them into contact, could be imagined combining to make a kind of cosmic musical orrery 'Yes, I suppose so,' I said. Then after a moment gazing at the infinite scatter of light and dark patterned over our heads she asked, 'is that why the piano keys are black and white?'

*     *     *

Tinctoris, whose *De Contrapuncto* of 1477 is usually thought of as the earliest treatise on Western polyphony, brought Boethian harmonies down to earth with a thump. '. . . No one shall make me believe that musical consonances arise through movements of the heavenly bodies, for they can only be produced by means of terrestrial instruments.' He described systematically the dos and don'ts that made the polyphony of his age a new music to his ears. Counterpoint – synonymous here with polyphony – he says 'arises when one tone is placed opposite another . . . If this combination or mixture sounds pleasant, it is called consonance; if, on the other hand, it sounds harsh and unpleasant, it is called dissonance.'

This remains more or less what I was taught: *polyphony*, the simultaneous sounding of two or more voices – *harmony*, the interplay of consonant and dissonant voices within a polyphony. And these two elements correspond to two axes: the horizontal pull of intertwining voices in time, and the vertical accumulation of the pitch of those voices at any given instant. These seem quite good concepts for a theoretical approach to European *written* music up to, say, the end of the 19th century when the notion of dissonance attenuates to the point of collapse. But they're limited in relation to performance because they ignore the questions every musician faces as he or she actually plays. *How* should the music sound? *When* should it sound (even the most precise score is only an approximate guide)? And, for contemporary musicians, (and for all improvisers and players of unscored music, who after all are instantaneous composers), *why* a certain sound and not another?

If Tinctoris could respond to the question what is it that makes a sound 'pleasing', he would surely reply that it's all laid out in his rules of counterpoint, rules which themselves conform to a particular vision of the way the world is ordered. Having no such clear frame of reference a contemporary musician *invents* a vision of the world in the choices he or she makes. In this sense the polyphonies of an epoch are a political mirror. How you choose to lay your voice into the texture of other voices reflects how you imagine they might all live together.

*     *     *

Here's something that John Cage's good friend Morton Feldman wrote about how sounds might live together:

Stockhausen asked me for my secret... and I said 'I don't have any secret, but if I do have a point of view, it's that sounds are very much like people. And if you push them, they push you back. So, if I have a secret: don't push the sounds around.' Karlheinz leans over to me and says: 'not even a little bit?'

And here's another thing that Feldman wrote: 'Polyphony sucks.'

*     *     *

I asked Francis what he thought polyphony was and he said, 'it's matter. If I build a house, then I make a polyphony.' As the French say, Francis likes a *bagarre*.

We were playing one evening and had a two hour drive to get to the venue. At one moment we passed through an inexplicably intricate one-way system and, irritated by the route he was obliged to take, he remarked in reply to something I'd said several kilometres further up the road, 'in any case, music is always hierarchic . . . there's always someone who directs.' I disagreed. 'If I'm playing with you,' I said, 'You don't direct me. I *choose* to go with you or else try to find another route. And then you make your own choice, to follow or not.' He denied that I had that sort of freedom.

'If you accompany singers, your role is defined by them.'
'I negotiate my role according to how they sing.'
'Voilà. You're *directed* by them.'
'No. Within the constraints they impose there are any
number of ways I might go.'
'You play G minor when you should play A minor, you're
wrong,' and then he swore as the traffic system made us turn
left where we wanted to turn right.

Later we stopped at a supermarket to get some petrol. On the
forecourt for a moment I began throwing pebbles against the
base of a lamp which responded with a lingering metallic ring.
It was, if you like, 'pleasing'. Fooling around with that noise, I
reflected that Francis is one of the few musicians I know who
would happily have improvised a piece on the spot to that sound.
*Music for accordina, streetlamp and pebbles.* In the hierarchy of
things, I like the irony that he's always obliged to explain what
an 'accordina' – his instrument – is, because he's the only person
in the world so far as I know who has spent his life trying to play
it and nobody recognises it. 'Is that a harmonica?' people say.

\*     \*     \*

'Naturally, as the lead voice, I might have shaped the performance,
but I had no wish to be a dictator. If the music itself did not
coax a response, I did not want one' (Bill Evans on the trio with
LaFaro and Motian).

\*     \*     \*

The eighth of Tinctoris' principles concerning polyphony states
that music should aim to be 'manifold', that is (I assume), voices
should be layered together with the maximum of variety. In this
respect the frogs score low since loudest-croaker-wins is a poor
way of differentiating an individual voice.

But as a reflection on *translation* . . . ?

Isn't translation a polyphonic art, since it layers one voice (an author's) into another (a translator's) and arguably many others out of history whose voices have shaped the languages we write and speak with? Isn't translation a way of weaving the variousness of different voices?

One of the joys of playing with musicians you love is that they translate your sounds into their own musical language so that you hear your own voice permanently re-voiced, or indeed anticipated. Evans said of LaFaro, 'Scott was incredible . . . about knowing where your next thought was going to be.' In the best ensembles the weave of musical ideas is translated into something of which the musicians individually could never have conceived.

*       *       *

And here's what another poet-musician friend said of polyphony. 'Polyphony is government by Unparliament.'

*       *       *

For Tinctoris, see, Knud Jeppesen, *Counterpoint: The Polyphonic Vocal Style of the 16th Century*, Dover, New York, 1992.
For Evans and LaFaro, see, Peter Pettinger, *Bill Evans: How My Heart Sings*, Yale UP, New Haven & London, 1998, pps. 113 -114.
Morton Feldman, *Give My Regards to Eighth Street*, ed. B.H.Friedman, Exact Exchange, Cambridge MA, 2000. 'Polyphony sucks' is a doodle reproduced on p.158.

# Three voices: Gerard Manley Hopkins, Dorothea Grünzweig, Derk Wynand

## I. Gerard Manley Hopkins, *translated by* Dorothea Grünzweig

### (Ashboughs)

Not of all my eyes see, wándering on the world,
Is anything a milk to the mind so, só sighs déep
Poetry to it, as a tree whose boughs break in the sky.
Say it is áshboughs: whether on a December day and furled
Fast or they in clammyish láshtender combs creep
Apart wide and new-nestle at heaven most high.
They touch heaven, tabour on it; how their talons sweep
The smouldering enormous winter welkin! May
Mells blue and snowwhite through them, a fringe and fray
Of greenery: it is old earth's groping towards the steep
                              Heaven whom she childs us by.

# (Eschenäste)

Nicht von dem, was meine Augen sehen, wandernd über die
   Welt,
Ist etwas eine Milch dem Geist so, so seufzt tief
Poesie in ihn, wie Bäume, deren Äste sich ins Blau wiegeln.
Sagen wir Eschenäste: ob an Dezembertagen und dicht
Gewickelt oder kriechend in klammig schmitzenlinden
   Zinken
Weit zerteilt, neu-nestend an dem Himmelshöchsten.
Schlagen den Himmel an, trommeln ihn; wie ihre Klauen
   striegeln
Das glimmende enorme Winterfirmament! Mai
Lindert Bläue und Schneeweiss durch sie, Gefetz, Gelitz
Von Grünerei: es ist der alten Erde Tasten Richtung steilen
   Himmel durch welchen sie uns kindert.

From *Geliebtes Kind der Sprache,(The Darling Child of Speech)*, G.M.Hopkins' poetry
translated and with comments by Dorothea Grünzweig, Edition Rugerup, 2009.
The original taken from *Gerald Manley Hopkins: The Major Works,* ed. Catherine
Phillips, Oxford University Press, 2002. The title appears in parentheses because
Robert Bridges, the poem's first publisher, assigned it.

## II. Dorothea Grünzweig, *translated by* Derk Wynand

### VON DEN FELDERN ERZÄHLT VJELL AM TELEFON
wie sie wellen schlagen

vom wehen und wogen der felder
weil die getreidekeimlinge die erde brachen

vom erschienenen heilenden regen der aufs tal
seine schilfernde trockenheit niedersprang

von den trauerschnäppern dass sich zwei fanden
ihr zissel- und zwieselflug nistwillig vor dem kasten
viel wolken darüber ihre trübe schwarzschwere
doch durch sie sich flechtend feine fädelungen

fast ein gefieder von licht
ich sag ich komm und komm am besten gleich

am frühen noch fahlen morgen
halt du auf jeden fall die von der nacht schon lassende

die matte dunkelheit in schach der mai
so mild doch überwindlich nicht wird dabei helfen

From *Die Auflösung*, Wallstein Verlag, Göttingen, 2008.

## ON THE PHONE VJELL TALKS OF THE FIELDS
the way they're making waves


of the fields' wafting and rocking
as the ground gave birth to grain sprouts

of the healing rain that's appeared and pounced
down onto the valley its flaking dryness

of the pied flycatchers that two have paired up
their zissel- and zwieselflight nesteager near the birdhouse

many clouds above it their bleak blackweight
but weaving through them fine threadings

almost a plumage of light
i'll come i say and best i come at once

in the early still pale morning
just make sure you keep in check the faint dark

already loosing its hold on night the month of may
so mild yet insurmountable will help won't it with that

## GEGEN MORGEN KALBTE DER SCHLAF
ein traum erschien mit einem see


sicheres frühlingszeichen
dehnte sich aus nahm das dorf

die ganze gemarkung in seine mitte
inselte sie und beschien sie mit blau

dafür wollt ich den namen finden
damit der traum sich nicht verflüchtige

*anrainer maiblau*
        *akkordeonbläue*
                *grosses gongendes gnadenblau*

umschloss die grünüberschüttete insel
nach schwerem heimsuchendem winter

umschloss die laube die aue die aub

From *Die Auflösung,* Wallstein Verlag, 2008.



## SLEEP CALVED TOWARD MORNING
a dream appeared with a lake


sure sign of spring
expanded took the village

the whole region into its middle
islanded it and shone blue on it

i tried to find the name for that
so the dream would not evaporate

*neighbouring mayblue*
*accordionblueness*
*grand gonging gracious blue*

surrounded the island showered in green
after this winter's harsh affliction

surrounded the arbour the eyot the ait

# III. Derk Wynand, *translated by* Dorothea Grünzweig

## Little Spring Songs

1.
Winter stops biting hard and deep,
the spring not yet sure where to set
its teeth, leaving us
these bad metaphors, the seasonal jazz —
wind instruments, puffs
of nothing much that determines
the music.
The going eases as we go:
otherwise, how could we contain all
this who knows how to say or sing
what's inside us, jawbone shattering,
chattering right into summer?
Not to mention put words to it:
erotics of spring,
the little green erections,
green nudge, green wink,
grass stains at the knee?

**2.**

First love, first shame,
first fear of expulsion
by the parent-god who forgets
to leave the porch light on.
These are memories, too,
not just metaphor, as Mandelstam
would have it, that the world is full of,
casting their green light
always back on the world,
words that direct us back
to the grasses,
the grasses themselves pointing
to all the kept and unkept promises
of their green
and what that amounts to:
pastures, psalms, a joyous singing.

**3.**

What's to explain? Spring
has arrived and brought
none of its cruelties. We talk
long into evening and keep
the sun on our skins. Yes,
we could call it habit
or pattern and live with that.
Last fall's horse apples
have built a good soil,
and the late winter's made
little difference: tulips, irides,
roses have survived and are thriving.
What was the question? The Arab
gelding's shedding his white coat
like a cat's. Why do I mention
cats when we don't have them?
You could probably answer that;
it's not a trick question.
Or urge me outside again (who,
now, is urging whom?) to watch

the sun burn the dew away
from the simple grass that covers
all the black soil and does so
without taking up much room.

From *Closer to Home,* Brick Books, London, Ontario, 1997

# Kleine Frühlingslieder

1.
Winter beisst nicht mehr fest und tief,
Frühling ist noch am Überlegen, wo
er die Zähne ansetzt und lässt uns
diese schlechten Bilder, Jazz der Jahreszeit –
Blasinstrumente, Luftstösse
von so gut wie Nichts,
das die Musik bestimmt.
Das Gehen wird beim Gehen sanfter:
wie könnten wir sonst all dies in uns halten,
und wer kann alles sagen oder singen,
was sich in uns befindet, wo doch der Kiefer
klappert, plappert bis in den Sommer hinein?
Geschweige denn dafür Worte finden:
Erotik des Frühlings,
die kleinen grünen Erektionen,
grüne Stupser, grünes Zwinkern,
Grasflecken auf dem Knie.

**2.**
Erste Liebe, erste Scham,
erste Angst vor Austreibung
durch den Eltern-Gott, der vergisst,
das Licht am Eingang anzulassen.
Dies sind Erinnerungen, auch,
und nicht nur Bilder, wie's Mandelstamm
sich wünschte, von denen die Welt voll ist,
sie werfen ihr grünes Licht
immer zurück auf die Welt,
Worte, die uns zu den Gräsern
zurücklenken,
und die Gräser selbst sind gerichtet auf
all die gehaltenen, gebrochenen Versprechen
von ihrem Grün
und auf was dies hinausläuft:
Weiden, Psalmen, ein freudiges Singen.


**3.**
Was muss erklärt werden? Frühling
kam an und brachte keine seiner
Grausamkeiten. Wir plaudern
lang in den Abend hinein und lassen
die Sonne auf unserer Haut. Ja,
wir könnten's Gewohnheit nennen
oder ein Muster und leben damit.
Die Pferdeäpfel des letzten Herbsts
bildeten einen guten Boden,
und der späte Winter hat nicht
viel bewirkt: Tulpen, Iride,
Rosen überlebten und stehen in Blüte.
Wie hiess die Frage? Der Araberwallach

schüttelt seinen weissen Mantel
wie eine Katze. Warum sprech ich
von Katzen, wenn wir keine haben?
Du könntest dies vielleicht beantworten;
es ist keine Trickfrage.
Oder mich drängen, wieder rauszugehen
(halt, wer drängt jetzt wen?) um zu sehen,
wie die Sonne den Tau wegsengt
vom schlichten Gras über all dem
schwarzen Boden und das schafft,
ohne dafür viel Platz zu brauchen.

*(We are grateful to Wallstein Verlag, Göttingen for allowing us to reprint Dorothea's poems.)*

# Régis Bonvicino and Antônio Moura
# Variations on Pound's 'In a Station
# of the Metro'
## *Translated by Stefan Tobler*

Régis Bonvicino is a major contemporary poet, a translator from English, and a judge. In addition, he is the founding editor of *Sibila*, a journal that makes a point of being international, including publishing English-language essays and translations. Its editorial committee members come from many countries and Charles Bernstein currently co-edits the magazine. Bonvicino has collaborated with and translated Charles Bernstein and Michael Palmer, and some of his earlier poetry is available in English translation in *Sky-Eclipse* (2000), published by Green Integer.

Antônio Moura is a poet and translator. His collections are *Dez* (1996), *Hong Kong & outros poemas* (1999), *Rio Silêncio* (2004) and *A sombra da ausência* (2009). His poems have appeared in many Brazilian journals and newspapers, as well as in a number of contemporary anthologies in Brazil and abroad, including *Nothing the Sun Could Not Explain: 20 Contemporary Brazilian Poets* (2nd edition; 2003).

The apparition of these faces in the crowd;
Petals on a wet, black bough.

Abruptos tiras ocultos na multidão;
Tiros na nuca, um corpo espúrio no chão.

— by Régis Bonvicino


*The apparition of these faces in the crowd;*
*Petals on a wet, black bough.*

Abrupt cops hide in the crowd;
Shot a man cops it, bogus body on the ground.

— translation by Stefan Tobler


**Numa estação do metrô,** *around*
*1916 d.c.,* a aparição das
faces na multidão, pétalas
num ramo escuro úmido,
dilata a pupila de Ezra,
enquanto outra turba
(a mesma?) se despetala:
um tiro (a esmo) desfolha
a bala a rosa da multidão,
numa estação do metrô,
*1998 d.c.*

— by Antônio Moura

**In a Station of the Metro,** *around*
*1916 AD,* the apparition of
these faces in the crowd, petals
on a black humid bough,
dilates Ezra's pupil,
while another throng
(same one?) de-petals:
a shot (astray) defoliates
the bullet the rose of the crowd,
in a station of the metro,
*1998 AD*

— translation by Stefan Tobler

## In a Station of the Metro

The apparition of these faces in the crowd;
Petals on a wet, black bough.

— the poem by Pound

### Translator's note

Here are three poems based on one, three coming out of one.
Not that they are some perfect trinity; they could be the start
of a series. Pound's 'In a Station of the Metro' is re-worked by
Moura in 'Numa estação do metrô', while Moura's poem as well
as Pound's appear to be the stimuli for Régis Bonvicino's 'The
apparition of these faces in the crowd'. You could say the two
later poems are riffing on the earlier one(s), you could also say
they are renga — being in the spirit of the Japanese renga tradition
of collaborative, accretive poetry, such as we find in the poems

of Sōgi (1421–1502) and Matsuo Bashō, and also – in Bonvicino's case – using its 5 and 7 syllabic units to compose the lines.

Contemporary Brazilian poetry is often very concise, compact. This pared-down tendency from the 1980s to recent years arises in part from the precise poetic constructions of João Cabral de Melo Neto and of Concrete Poetry, and is called 'constructivist' poetry in Brazil. Régis Bonvicino (b. 1955) has been its most influential exemplar, although his poetry is not limited to such a definition. Antônio Moura is a younger poet (b. 1964) whose early work in particular shows the influence of the constructivist poetics, as can be seen in this poem 'Numa estação do metrô' from his second collection *Hong Kong* (1999).

The first four lines of Moura's 'Numa estação do metrô' cite a Portuguese translation of Pound's poem 'In a Station of the Metro' and intercut the quote with (in his original poem:) *'around / 1916 d.c'* ('d.c.' corresponding in Portuguese to our 'a.d.', *anno domini*). The reconfigured lines and insertion break up the syllabic form of Pound's poem. Pound's poem itself plays with its antecedents, it is an inversion of the Japanese haiku's syllabic count 5-7-5 with its two lines of 12 (the sum of 7 and 5) and 7 syllables.

Moura's poem breaks the Imagist beauty of petals on a bough with a violent shooting on the metro *'1998 d.c.'*. I asked Moura if this referred to a particular incident, but he said that 'it does not refer to any specific death, it was a fictitious vision, a kind of poetic cinematography, with cut / montage, a plot and characters'. Yet now it seems like a strange case of life imitating art, in view of the killing in the London underground of the Brazilian Jean Charles de Menezes 22 July 2005 by British police who mistook him for a terror suspect, two weeks after the 7 July bombings in London.

In Bonvicino's later poem, published in 2007 in his collection *Página órfã* (Orphan Page) it is of course impossible not to relate the poem to the death of de Menezes. Bonvicino's poem re-works Pound's and Moura's poem, and returns to the metrics of the Japanese tradition which we find in Pound's poem. According to the rules of Portuguese verse, both the Portuguese-language lines in Bonvicino's poem are of 12 syllables (the second one being divided into 5 syllables before the comma, 7 after it). There is not so much a sense of a sequence of poems, but of an increasing polyphony. Each poem looks both backwards and forwards, and the sense of circularity is only increased by Moura's poem preceding de Menezes' killing.

# Reza Baraheni
## 'Daf'
### *Translated by Stephen Watts with the author*

Reza Baraheni is one of the major contemporary Persian writers, as a poet, novelist and critic. He was imprisoned under the Shah and was banned by and had to seek exile from the Islamic Republic. His prison poems *God's Shadow* were published in translation by Indiana UP in 1976 and his essays *Crowned Cannibals: Writings On Repression In Iran* were also published in the US and widely read at the time. A number of his novels have been translated into French over the past fifteen years and published in Paris by Fayard. The range of his concerns, as well as his constant anti-imperialism and resistance to oppression, has not endeared him to any of his country's regimes. He has lived in exile in Toronto for many years and is a former president of PEN Canada.

'Daf' reflects not only his Persian but also particularly his Azeri roots: he was born in Tabriz (in 1935) and thus is much concerned with Azeri, Turkic & Kurdish cultures, as well as more mainstream Persian themes. A daf is a round drum (in many ways not unlike a bodhran) played at times to ecstasy and to sharp climax. Baraheni's poem dances linguistically through its pages and I've attempted to measure this in the English translation and to reflect its rhythms and space: the opening, for instance, seeks to convey the circular shape of a daf. Much of the language and layout reverberates with Azeri and Kurdish energies, themes and rhythms. It is a volcanic poem of air, rock and breath, plunging from its title down to its very last word.

# Daf

Beating the daf, shaking it
beating it, breaking it out in shake music, beating
the midnight moon beating the daf moon's night in the
ecstatic bursting of laughter in the *ha* of the hallelu-jah
in the turbulent rolling of struck thunder
On drum days when the shining in the outburst of Shirin's
dream is the music that Farhad was aching for
Deafen down the daf when the belt of thunder of the future
drums out truths from its circle & strikes itself in just
where we need it to strum it out again
Daf intravening daf moon into moaning moon & there-
fore in its oven mouth-baked – the white round bread
of the sky, the daf of the soul, the music of
the tight skin around the
spirit's dream

Now night will never sense silence again
and after these circles of turbulence
I'll not sleep for a geology of un-numberable years
Here night swells on rim edges of drums and bells –
the daf's white moon : flick it from your wrist
but do not throw it away
I'm telling you take this & affidavit it in the juice & leisure
of the moment : do not I beg you leave it
alone

Kurd of the spirit
Lank-haired
Eye dervished by squinting
Eyebrow pulled across toward miracles
You poppy-eyed
Sun-lipped
Sneak-thief of a thousand fires You bursting into laughter where
copper melts into fever and the gold of the *daf daf daf* opens
up the oven of my body : do not give up this music

Planets of the daf
are pulsing in the swallow gardens
*daf daf de daf de daf daf*

Blood is dripping
from this poem as from your eyes
*daf daf de daf*

A woman running on the titanium coast screams
'god god god why have you forgotten the sky of Teheran'
the daf-given golden face of the full moon gleams
in the face of the woman

*daf daf de daf da daf*
*daf daf de daf da daf*
*daf daf de daf da daf*

You
My beloved
You sky
Man-Woman
of the spirit
Mandala secret
Opium-eyed
*daf daf da daf* of the oven of my body
Kurd of the spirit

You struck Kirkuk with the strength of your voice
on Kurghau-Gaaf
*daf daf da daf*
*daf daf da daf*
You simurged the Alborz mountains reviving their rock spirits
with the drum glint of this trance
*daf daf da daf*
*daf daf da daf da daf*
Shake awake you star ancestor of drums from their sleep
Darling simurg be violent
Startle everyone
*daf daf da daf*
*daf daf da daf da daf*
*daf daf da daf da daf daf daf da daf*


When in the ruby desert
the drumbell of the daf is playing
rise up in me and on my shoulders
& above my heart    breasts    *daf*
it is the jump of blood that is pumping
judas tree fingered with purple
with its fist of perfume & honeys
it is the *daf daf da daf* that is beating
I am the coastline and the waves
are the *daf* beats of sounds pounding
I am the earth and it is the hooves
of herd beasts drumming out
the heartbeats of
the daf

The ancient spirit of Ghonia is a fire beneath the earth, Ghonia that
has blossomed on the earth's shoulders as judas tree and tulip
It is the dream drum of the dear daf that is beating
on Ghonia

O you young youth
You Urmavi
You inbreath of breaking speech
It is the daf's *daf* breaking
on Maulavi


On scorched meadows
Tabriz has inscribed
Shams
You Urmavi
You young Babylon of the oldest tongues
The ancient spirit of Ghonia is a fire beneath the earth, Ghonia that
has blossomed on the earth's shoulders as judas trees and tulips
It is the drum dream of the drawn daf that is beating
on Ghonia


Winds blow out the blast edges
and gust-cliffs of Azeri peaks and pour into lakes
where nomad herders with their herds make fire and bivouac
it is the ache and crack of the *daf* that is beating
Suns from early-risen mountain peaks light up waiting turrets of
high rock pastures further west
This Zoroaster of the mountain culture is among us
the drum and clash and cluster of the *daf*
beating on the roof

Camel's milk
On the roof of the moon
Carafe of wine
On the tip of the tongue
Swirl of the skin on the daf that is beating
Sea of lilies painted on our ceilings
It is the dizzy dance of the daf that is beating
rippled in its core-line stem
It is the dancing planet that is beating
It is the dancing plummet *da daf*
It is the dancered dizzied *daf*
It is the *daf daf da daf* that is beaten
and beating


You young youth
You throat that
is kissable
Let me kiss you
Iris
Young mouth
You fist of honeys
Perfume and honeys
Kissable throat
You iris


My drum moon whirling round the world
behind the dancing daf
full moon
full moon
full moon
It is the daf that is beating out *da daf*
eyes wet with honey
wine carafe
waterfall

My moon daf whirling round the world
My round daf
My woman-man
My asylum of miracles & margins


Beating the daf beating its music out under the moon
at midnight night    of Zoroaster    of mountain culture among us
in the ecstatic breaking of the laughter of the *ha* of hallelu-jah
in the turbulent bursts of its struck thunder
my daf moon is whirling round the world
circles of its light haloes of the planets of its heads
from the sky and its bewilderment of necks
from the shoulders of its shadow
the head flies off
the head jumps free
the daf beats the hand
the hand beats the daf
it is the sound of the daf being slapped
that knocks off our human heads
*daf daf da daf daf*

Young youth
iris
throat that is kissable
you head beheader
it is the sound of the daf
that knocks off our heads
Are you struck dumb
are you headless
yet

Stump red & severed orb
blood rump & miracle of distant dirt
calve along the colour skein dazed in the *daf da daf daf*
that's dawning in the crazed days of the mind where
thousands of stars also call out
it is the *daf daf da daf* that is beating
and these stars are
in the planets of the head and in
fragrances of fast-flowing rains and in the confluence of many
taut skins in the *daf daf da daf* that is being out-breathed:
drum like velvet that within its sheen
has dervished all the love
of its frenzied planets


Let me melt me in the revolving
of the madness of the frenzied *daf* your crazy
*daf* where what can you do aieeee . . .
Let me make myself in the circle of the madness crazy daf
aieeee . . . let me meet me in the whirled of the madness
of your frenzy *daf* your crazied *daf* where what
can you do aieeee . . .
Aieeee . . .
Aieeee . . .
Let me melt myself
in the revolving of the madness crazy *daf* aieeee . . .


Aieeee . . .

# W.D. Jackson
# German children's rhymes

The time is past – or should be – when children's poetry belonged in the 'nursery', as one of the ways in which little children should not be heard. In German as in English, its voice is that of a child, of course. But children are confronted by questions as serious in their way as those of their parents, and the best of their rhymes reflect this. Possibly because of the status of Grimms' *Märchen*, traditional German rhymes have been treated with the greatest respect by artists as varied as Gustav Mahler, Günther Grass, Walter Benjamin and H.M. Enzensberger... Some of my versions are closer than others to the anonymous German on which they are based, but since – like children's rhymes everywhere – the originals are found for the most part in more than one form, rewriting seems a valid procedure in this case:

> Mrs Fox is in her lair,
> Weeping and wailing it isn't fair
> That her coat is red:
> Mr Fox is dead.

*

# The Crooked Hunchback

If I go into our garden,
When I want to hide or play,
There's a crooked little hunchback
Who keeps getting in my way.

If I go into our kitchen,
When I want to ask for more,
There's a crooked little hunchback
Knocks my porridge on the floor.

When I go into our cellar
Where it's always damp and dark,
There's a crooked little hunchback
Puts the light out for a joke.

If I go into my bedroom,
When it's time to make my bed,
There's a crooked little hunchback
Laughs until he's nearly dead.

When I go into the church
Where I sing or kneel and pray,
There's a crooked little hunchback
Who says what he said today:

*Little child, I beg of you,*
*Pray for the crooked hunchback too.*

\*

# The Hungry Child

Mother, oh mother, I can't get my breath,
Give me some bread, I'm starving to death.
Be brave and don't cry now, my little man,
Tomorrow we'll sow as fast as we can.

And when they'd sowed the corn,
The child was still forlorn.
Mother, oh mother, I can't get my breath,
Give me some bread, I'm starving to death.
Don't cry now, have patience, my little man,
We're cutting the corn as fast as we can.

And when they'd cut the corn,
The child was still forlorn.
Mother, oh mother, I can't get my breath,
Give me some bread, I'm starving to death.
Be patient, be patient, my little man,
We're threshing the corn as fast as we can.

And when they'd threshed the corn,
The child was still forlorn.
Mother, oh mother, I can't get my breath,
Give me some bread, I'm starving to death.
Be patient and wait now, my little man,
We're grinding the corn as fast as we can.

And when they'd ground the corn,
The child was still forlorn.
Mother, oh mother, I can't get my breath,
Give me some bread, I'm starving to death.
Wait, oh wait, my little man,
We're baking the bread as fast as we can.

But when they'd baked the bread,
The child was dead.

*

An angel sat on a branch in a tree
With a chicken for you and a chicken for me.
He would have liked to gut them,
But had no knife to cut them.
A knife dropped down from the clouds above
And chopped the angel's head right off.
The milk-maid ran to the barber's shop
But no one was there to bandage it up.
In the kitchen the cat was sleeping,
From the window a mouse was peeping.
On the roof the chickens – still unplucked –
Ruffled their feathers and squawked and clucked.

*

## About Schlaraffenland

Schlaraffenland's a wondrous place
Where lazy lumps can feed their face
Behind Rice Pudding Hill.
But if you want to get there, you
Must munch much more than your fill.

The hill is more than three miles long –
Just chomp and chew, you can't go wrong.
Unless you become too sick,
You'll find the houses there all built
Of cake instead of brick.

The fence around the garden is
Made up of huge fried sausages,
And anyone who wants
Can eat them, and the cake-house too –
There are no Do's and Don'ts.

Roast geese and ducks and pigeons fly
Like real live birds across the sky.
Nothing you've seen can match it.
And if you want to eat one, all
You've got to do is catch it.

Sometimes they land on the kitchen table,
While roasted porkers there are able
To run around with knives
Stuck in their tender meat – to carve it.
You'll have the time of your lives!

There honey falls instead of rain,
And almond flakes snow slowly down.
Doughnuts, not shut pine-cones,
Grow on the trees in Lollipop Wood.
Milk-streams have chocolate stones.

All sorts of women, children, men,
Lie idling there. Whoever can
Do nothing's made a lord.
The laziest of the lot's their king.
His fat knights were born bored.

Now, if you'd like to set off, but
Are still unsure which way to trot,
Ask anyone who's blind.
The deaf and dumb will also tell
You where to go, you'll find.

*Red, white and blue,*
*A shame it's not true.*

*

Pitchy patchy Peter
Hides behind the heater,
Darning socks and shining shoes,
Till the old cat miaows and mews:
    She's a greedy eater!
Eats the shine and eats the shoe,
Then she eats up Peter too.
Eats the shoe and eats the shine,
Eats your dinner, then eats mine.

*

A fox sat in the green plum-tree
Plucking yellow plums for tea.
I said he'd better give me one,
He said he'd throw me down a stone.
I took up my white stick instead –
And knocked off his red head.

*

Fixy foxy, foxy fix,
Don't you chase my hen or chicks!
If you harm my chicks or hen,
May the cuckoo chase *you* then –
On the kitchen table put you,
Gut you like a fish and cut you
With his beak in very many
Bits no bigger than a penny!

*

Mr Crow, don't mop and mow,
Grieving still for Mrs Crow
    In the rain and mud.
Can't afford a pair of boots,
And you'll spatter your black suit
    In the rain and mud.
If you'd also lost a leg,
One boot you could beg
    In the rain and mud.
But you're proud as well as poor,
Stalking round outside my door
    In the rain and mud.

\*

Ladybird, ladybird, fly past my door.
Your mother's gone to Hamburg town,
Your father's gone to war.
Hamburg town is all burned down.
Ladybird, fly past my door.

\*

Where have you been all winter, my son?
Where did you live and what have you done?
I built a house in Schlampampenland.
That's good. What's good? It was built on sand,
And a wild pig came and knocked it down.
That's bad. What's bad? I took my gun,
And shot the pig for its sausage-meat.
That's good. What's good? Two feet and four feet
Stole my meat in the thick of the night.
That's bad. What's bad? I cut off their flight.
Four feet is now my friend for life,
And two feet my wife.

# Salman Masalha
# 'The Song'
## *Translated by Vivian Eden with the author*

Salman Masalha was born in 1953 in al-Maghar, an Arab town in the Galilee, and has lived in Jerusalem since 1972. He studied at the Hebrew University and holds a Ph.D. degree in classical Arabic literature, for which he wrote a thesis on mythological aspects of classical Arabic poetry. He taught Arabic language and literature at the Hebrew University of Jerusalem, and served as co-editor of the Concordance of Early Arabic Poetry.

He writes in both Arabic and Hebrew and publishes translations into both languages. He has published seven volumes of poetry; his articles, columns, poems and translations have appeared in newspapers, journals and anthologies in both Arabic and Hebrew as well as in various other languages. Some of his Arabic and Hebrew poems have been performed to music and recorded by leading Israeli and Palestinian musicians. For his book *Ehad Mikan* (In Place), He was awarded the President's Prize for Hebrew poetry. Read his prose and more poetry at the multi-lingual blog *http://salmaghari-en.blogspot.com/*

# The Song

*The Arab's Speech*

Every time I say I'm hungry
a military genius hands me a fishing pole
and sends me to catch some fish in the desert,
but I hook only scales.
And as I don't drink sand,
I can't pass my water. Moreover
I suffer from constipation.
And as I am hungry, and truly love life,
I eat my toes, because I so regret
I agreed to go out fishing
in murky sands.


*The Jew's Speech*

Every time I say I'm hungry
a political genius sends me to drink
the sea water. Then I pass,
with my water, a fish without scales.
I am unable to dish it up on my table.
It's strictly banned by religious law.
And as I am hungry, and truly love life,
I throw it back into the sea, where it dies of thirst
for I drank up all its water first.
I laugh out of sorrow, as in my current state
I can't even die
of laughter.

*The Silent Majority's Speech*

Death to the hungry!
Death to the hungry!


*The Fish's Speech*

Silence is boring!
Silence is boring!
If you don't stop,
I won't talk
and I won't pass water
any more.


*The Poet's Speech*

Enough! When
will this song end?

# John Greening
# 'To the Sun'
# After Akhenaten

## Akhenaten's *Hymn to the Sun*

Akhenaten may be best known today as the subject of Philip Glass's minimalist opera. But his place in history stems from a decision to shift from worship of the old gods approved by the Theban Priesthood to a strictly monotheistic religion focused on the solar disc or 'Aten'. Despite the many books written on him and his consort, Nefertiti, little of substance is known about this 18th dynasty pharaoh because the Priests of Amen effectively erased the heretic from history. But in the remains of his palace at Amarna, among the extraordinary informal images of pharaonic family life, a 'Hymn to the Sun' is several times inscribed. It is the most celebrated piece of Ancient Egyptian literature (Glass uses it in his opera) and has long been attributed to Akhenaten himself. The Hymn's catalogue of praise for the sun's life-giving power has an incantatory quality, reminiscent of the Psalms – particularly Psalm 104. This makes it quite unyielding to read and hard to 'translate' into anything other than a Biblical register. Since leaving Upper Egypt (at least a dynasty ago), I have occasionally tinkered with the Hymn and tried to transmute it into something readably modern, something less monophonic. Perhaps it was a spell of unwonted English summer heat that

fertilized this strange and sidewinding new version in me, rather
as 'your serpent of Egypt is bred, now, of your mud by the
operation of your sun' (Lepidus's drunken suggestion to Antony).
'To the Sun' is very much a Lowell-style 'imitation' in which I
have used elements of other translators' versions (I do not read
hieroglyphics) to create a solar poem, whose source is Akhenaten,
but which casts a few contemporary shadows.

# To The Sun

*after Akhenaten*

Glorious as the hills in the east now
it spills light, at sea level.

Feast from its prehistoric silver
plate, these dateless riches,

released at last from the tyranny
of sunlessness, of light starvation.

A distant fact, an elephant-in-the-room
dictator, retiring, then flaring

beyond the trace of any probe:
we forget you, plugged into our

electric shadow, drowning in dazzling
gloom, asleep under sodium,

among coiled, low-energy dreams:
we dare not look at one another

unless it's through a screen, strangers
steal our identities, friends become

spot, rash, stroke... feverish,
we forget that you have even set

and are rising already over Al-Hadr,
the swastika lands, the dragon cities,

the thorny paths of Wuriupranili.
But dawn comes, though we ignore its

sacred polyphony, an alarm call
from *Star Trek*, the kettle boiling, cars

as they tick, the radio chatter:
it will be hot, there will be flights

towards your smile, which says *I am here*
*behind ceiling tiles, rafters,*

*insulation, slates and slatey rain-*
*clouds, beyond volcanic ash.*

*Bathe, bask, bare all, ride*
*your chariot, let us be gas guzzlers,*

*my fingers touching that prominence*
*to bless your bones and infiltrate*

*the days, the years.* And do not raise
the subject *x*, the item *gamma*

as we apply the UVF to our children
by the sea, and do not listen to what follows

the pips (the fission, ozone, carbon
dioxide, fusion and confusion).

Let the chick come unmutated
from the egg. Let it come crowing.

Crops must be warm. We must put up
with polytunnels. Keep the cliffs secure,

till desert and its wildfires stagger
over the horizon. Respect the winter,

don't give your smouldering horses
rein such as will hurl us all

to a solar arc. You watched us rise.
Don't let us be washed away

in rolling news. We do not understand
the gravity of your stare, the currents

above or below, we simply know
time and tide, it never rains,

make hay, the switch that says on/
off. We block, we quit the field.

The turbines begin to turn, but you
are the only god we believe in, even here

in East Anglia: as on the West Bank.

# Han Dong
# Two poems
## *Translated by Nicky Harman*

Born 1961, Nanjing, Han Dong is an important avant-garde poet as well as an essayist, fiction writer, editor of non–official poetry journals and blogger. His first novel, 扎根, was translated as *Banished!* (UHP, 2009) and long-listed for the Man Asian Literary Prize. Han Dong's poems break new ground with their repudiation of high culture and other heroics. He creates subtle, deceptively 'simple' verse using popular [扎根] language and takes pleasure in puncturing pomposity and debunking political myths. His poems are also funny, rude, often sexy, and highly visual. In 2009, he won the judges' prize at an independent poetry festival held in Yunnan, China.

# A phone call from Dalian

A phone call from Dalian. She was not even
My former lover. It had no purpose. The call
Simply told her phone number. A woman
Made me think back to a kind of face popular three years
    ago.

She was just married, in a new house smelling of fresh paint
Which went perfectly with the stately furniture
(Including the phone she'd personally picked)
Was it perhaps just from curiosity (like a young cat)
That, as she fiddled with her husband's possessions, she
    happened
To dial my number?

Were Dalian's ancient waves lapping outside her window?
Was there that rock, still insisting on
Its stirring image? If, many years after – but not too long –
She were to call again, from middle age, she would certainly
Have learnt about life. Thirty years later
There would just be waves, in my right ear
I would not even hear her harsh, she-animal breathing.

1993

Taken from 爸爸在天上看我 [Dad's looking down on me from the
sky], Hebei Education Press, 2002

## 来自大连的电话

一个来自大连的电话，她也不是
我昔日的情人。没有目的。电话
仅在叙述自己的号码。一个女人
让我回忆起三年前流行的一种容貌

刚刚结婚，在飘满油漆味儿的新房
正适应和那些庄严的家具在一起
（包括一部亲自选购的电话）
也许只是出于好奇（象年轻的母猫）
她在摆弄丈夫财产的同时，偶尔
拨通了给我的电话？

大连古老的海浪是否在她的窗前？
是否有一块当年的礁石仍在坚持
感人的形象？多年以后－－不会太久
如果仍有那来自中年的电话，她一定
学会了生活。三十年后
只有波涛，在我的右耳
我甚至听不见她粗重的母兽的呼吸

# Some people don't like to talk

Some people don't like to talk
They're not dumb or introverted
They only speak when necessary
Just courtesies
Just floating on the surface of talk
They spend their whole lives like that
It can be summed up very briefly
Some people live their lives like epitaphs
Long years but the words are short and simple
Upright as tomb stones
They stand soberly before us.

2004


## 一些人不爱说话

一些人不爱说话

既不是哑巴，也不内向

只说必要的话

只是礼节

只浮在说话的上面

一生就将这样过去

寥寥数语即可概括

一些人活着就像墓志铭

漫长但言词简短

像墓碑那样伫立着

与我们冷静相对

# Luis Amorim de Sousa
## 'Bellini and Pablo as well'
*Translated by Anthony Rudolf with the author*

'Bellini and Pablo as well' is the title poem of the latest poetry collection published by Luís Amorim de Sousa (Assírio & Alvim, Lisbon 2007). It was also chosen to conclude the memoir which the author dedicated to the Portuguese poet Alberto de Lacerda (1928–2007), his friend of many years. As well as being a portrait of Alberto de Lacerda, the poem seeks to describe the nature of their friendship enjoyed in different city scenarios, a friendship fed by common interests and lateral connections. It was written for Alberto on the occasion of his 70th birthday, which the two poets celebrated together in London.

Luís Amorim de Sousa, poet and memoirist, was born in Angola in 1937. After a Lisbon childhood he lived in Mozambique and, for most of his adult life, in London and Washington DC. He lives currently in Portugal where he manages the Alberto de Lacerda estate. Wherever he goes, he hears Whitman's 'continual echoes from the Thames'. Both poets worked for the BBC Portuguese Service for a number of years.

Anthony Rudolf, who has co-translated Luis Amorim de Sousa's poem with the author, knew Alberto de Lacerda for more than forty years and co-translated a number of his poems.

Alberto de Lacerda's 77 *Poems* was published in London in 1955, in a bilingual edition with translations by Arthur Waley, who also wrote the preface. In fact this was the first of his twelve Portuguese collections. A later bilingual volume, *Selected Poems*, was published by the University of Texas at Austin in 1969. Among Alberto de Lacerda's translators were Octavio Paz, Christopher Middleton, Nathaniel Tarn, David Wevill and Michael Hamburger, all contributors to *MPT*.

## Bellini and Pablo as well

Alberto Alberto
how numbers can be deceptive

now you are seventy
three times that in experience
but only half in your heart

        say nothing I already know
you will reply
           quoting Yeats:
'the heart grows old'

but not yours
not your heart

it flowers every day
even in bad weather

     and how bad weather upsets you

the phone rings
            it's your voice:

        have you seen this dreadful weather?
        it never ends
                    it's unbearable

but the conversation flows
and your inner climate mellows
it becomes sunny resplendent

you are unusual that way
and in many other ways

your fish and spaghetti
is unbelievable

        – does Alberto really cook?

and how you love using capers
you conjure up little shops to buy them
you conjure up everything
Victoria Square
                    what a find
Paris in the heart of London

and Blake's baptismal font
and poets who have never published
and all those art galleries in Mayfair

        I think that they are there for you
        just for you
        and your delight

there goes the phone
the telephone has become
essential for both of us

ring ring
it's you from afar
London Boston New York:

    I have just come back from MoMA
    you have to see that show

but first
your recommendations:

            go early
            no time to waste
            the exhibition is vast
            you have to concentrate

and then comes a 'conversete'
        your word for chat
        ours now
        interrupted by endless divagations

because as you have said
and written in a poem
that led Octavio Paz to write another
*conversation is divine*

and you are right

but sometimes you turn sombre
passing clouds    shadows
          exile
                  so many exiles
so many
no one can even imagine

and other times one calls
and your phone rings on and on
and you take forever to answer:

   I did not hear a thing
   I was listening to music

you explain later on
and then:

do you have a moment?

your moments go on for ever
the listener picks up noises
a gentle cough
shuffling steps

and then your voice once again:

   do you mind?
   do you have the patience
   to listen to a poem I wrote
   earlier today at the Picasso Café?

of course I have
what a thought
you make me think of Bandeira
and his poem for black Irene

wonderful Manuel Bandeira
wonderful friend of yours

so many friends
so many friendships

and ours that keeps on growing
but always remains unchanged
that covers different epochs with the toast:
Viva Bellini
Bellini and Pablo as well

that is local inter-city
inter-continental too
and I now dare to ask

do you have the patience for this?

it is a poem of friendship
written for you
on September the twentieth
by your friend
more than a friend
a brother
                          Luís

# Nasos Vayenas
# Five poems
### *Translated by Richard Berengarten and Paschalis Nikolaou*

Nasos Vayenas was born in the northern Greek city of Drama, in 1945. Following studies in Greek and Italian literature at the universities of Athens and Rome respectively, he completed an MA in literary translation at the University of Essex before writing his Ph.D. thesis on George Seferis at Cambridge University (1974-1979). Upon its subsequent publication in Greek, *The Poet and the Dancer* was acclaimed as a key statement on the Nobel Laureate's poetics.

In Vayenas's first book of poems, *Field of Mars* (1974), rhythmical patterns of Greek conversation combine in staccato sentences and phrases to produce tightly controlled 'free-form' poems. Already evident here is a sharp ear for intonation, innuendo and irony, all of which mark Vayenas out as a leading member of the 'Generation of the Seventies'. Terseness and irony remain constants throughout his *oeuvre* as he moves firstly to the 'verset' (in *Biography,* 1978) and then to forms more strongly marked by traditional rhythms and rhymes, including, for example, sonnets, in books such as *Dark Ballades and Other Poems* (2001) and his latest collection, *In the Isle of the Blest* (2010).

Concurrent with this direction, Vayenas's critical writings plead for a 're-enchantment of poetic discourse'. Indeed, the incessant dialogue between Vayenas's critical and lyrical voices permeates the work of a writer who is also Professor of Literary Theory and Criticism at the University of Athens. The simultaneous publication, in 1989, of the book of essays *Poetry and Translation* and a hybrid collection entitled *Flyer's Fall*, in which original poems converse with translations of a number of Anglophone and other modernists is perhaps the clearest example of poetry, translation and criticism consistently engaging through the contact points of a rich ensemble of writers and traditions. Nor has dialogue stopped there. As editor, Vayenas's *Conversing with Cavafy* (2000) has gathered an anthology of Cavafy-inspired poems from around the world. As translator, he has 'returned' Richard Berengarten's *Black Light: Poems in Memory of George Seferis* (2005, reviewed in *MPT* 3/5) to the Greek language.

Given the poet's characteristic inhabitation of multiple voices and modes, a key to the editing of his forthcoming *The Perfect Order: Selected Poems 1974-2010*, due from Anvil Press later this year, has been inclusion of versions by twelve translators, often in collaboration, thus allowing for a multiplicity of interpretations, timbres, and accents.

PN

## Torment

Wrong again in my metaphors.
Words elude me. Like betrayers
they tumble, like pieces of silver.
My lines give me away.
They have a will of their own.
They distort my personal vision.
They brazenly conjure decadent poets.

And yet the first words came out right.
The first line was quite perfect
in getting the feelings across.
But too soon
it got contaminated
by the memory of some
awful foreign poems.


(*from* Field of Mars, 1974)
*Translated by Richard Berengarten and Paschalis Nikolaou*




## Roxane's knees


It's hardly an essential component of eternal truth that you
should wear high mauve heels tipped with little gold rings.
Or that you should strive to pull out your most gorgeous
limbs fom the very teeth of time. Green leaves clatter down,
covering the earth. There are more things to be seen on the
ground than could ever be imagined. It occurs to me: if death
does exist, it's mainly because of his longing to overturn the
natural order of things. Give me your hand. Time isn't a liar
and out of all the things he passes judgement on, perhaps
something may get left

on your skin, some tiny snippet of immortality.


(*from* Roxane's Knees, 1981)
*Translated by Richard Berengarten & Paschalis Nikolaou*

## *Barbarous Odes*, XVI

The thirst for heaven is something I don't understand.
And no, my brow has never touched the stars.
As for azaleas (what kind of word is that)
they don't do anything for me.

A cloud from 1978 drifts past.
A strong wind is blowing in from
the future. Once upon a time night
was mother of the universe. Now

she's a grey rag hanging out
in some sleazy corner of Attica. What
I keep seeing in mirrors is an unpolished
translation of myself.

A dream: gently, blue burial urns
tumble into my chest. In the lap of time
half-naked, curls a curvy blonde
plucking petals from a black daisy.

(*from* Barbarous Odes, 1992)
*Translated by Richard Berengarten and Paschalis Nikolaou*

# Triantafyllos Moraitis

I left behind me ten collections of poetry,
five for the many and five for the few,
with god-given lines, that trace
the boundaries of zero.
The many did not read them,
the few did not understand them.
Still unread, and past understanding,
even though I do not live, I hope.

(*from* Garland, 2004)
*Translated by Paschalis Nikolaou*

# Cavafy

The multicoloured paper masks you donned
and year in, year out, changed afresh each day,
hid wrinkles, ironed their evidence away,
saved you from scorn within your demi-monde.

But only when you put by masks for good
did you see in the naked glass your face
and, meeting Time's eyes straight there, realise
that Time craves flesh, not John the Baptist's food.

But now your flesh is word, and your word's power,
nourished by Time, lays bare the human soul:
its majesties, its horrors, its decays.

And not just that. Your word lays bare the ways
that the soul is what a poem's lines reveal:
sucking the nipple, no mere pacifier.


(from *On the Isle of the Blest*, 2010)
*Translated by Richard Berengarten*


(all from *The Perfect Order: Selected Poems 1974–2010*, edited by
Richard Berengarten and Paschalis Nikolaou – forthcoming
from Anvil Press Poetry, December 2010)

Vyacheslav Kupriyanov
'Song of Odysseus'
*Translated by Dasha C. Nisula*

A poet, prose writer, translator, and critic, Vyacheslav Kupriyanov
was born in Novosibirsk, Russia, in 1939. He completed his
studies in Moscow where he currently lives and works. Over a
long and successful career Kupriyanov has published nine books
of poetry and prose, most of which have been translated into
many European languages. An anthology of his translations of
Austrian, German, Swiss and American poets was published in
Moscow by the Raduga Press in 2009.

## Song of Odysseus

When my ship comes in,
A song will come ashore with me,
To which till then only the sea was listening,
For the song was competing with the call of the sirens.
It will have only moist vowel sounds
That sound that way in the pale translation
From the language of roaming to the language of mooring:

I love you with the hoarse cry of the seagulls,
With the scream of the eagles, flying toward the scent of
   Prometheus' liver,
With the thousand year silence of the sea turtle,
With the click of the sperm whale that wants to be a roar,
With the pantomime, executed by the tentacles of the
   octopus,
Before which all seaweeds stand on end.

I love you with all my body coming from the sea,
With all its rivers, tributaries of the Amazon and the
   Mississippi,
With all those deserts, which think themselves seas,
You can hear their sand sift through my desiccated throat.

I love you with all my heart, lungs and pupil of my eye,
I love you with the earth's crust and the star-studded sky,
With the fall of waterfalls and the conjugation of verbs,
I love you with the invasion of Europe by the Huns,
With the Hundred Years War and the Mongolian Horde,
With the uprising of Sparta and the Great Migration,
With Alexander's column and the Tower of Pisa,
With the speed of the Gulf Stream warming the North Pole.

I love you with the letter of the law of gravity
And the verdict of the death penalty,
Unto the death penalty through the eternal fall
Into your bottomless Bermuda triangle.

## ПЕСНЬ ОДИССЕЯ

Когда мой корабль причалит к берегу,
Вместе со мной сойдет на берег песня,
Её прежде слушало только море,
Где она соперничала с зовом сирен.
В ней будут только влажные гласные звуки,
Которые так звучат в бледном переводе
С языка скитаний на язык причала:

Я люблю тебя охрипшим криком морских чаек,
Клекотом орлов, летящих на запах печени Прометея,
Тысячеликим молчаньем морской черепахи,
Писком кашалота, который хочет быть ревом,
Пантомимой, исполненной щупальцами осьминога,
От которой все водоросли встают дыбом.

Я люблю тебя всем моим телом вышедшим из моря,
Всеми его реками, притоками Амазонки и Миссисипи,
Всеми пустынями, возомнившими себя морями,
Ты слышишь, как их песок пересыпается в моем пересохшем горле.

Я люблю тебя всем сердцем, легкими и зеницей ока,
Я люблю тебя земной корой и звездным небом,
Падением водопадов и спряжением глаголов,
Я люблю тебя нашествием гуннов на Европу,
Столетней войной и татаро-монгольским игом,
Восстанием Спартака и Великим переселением народов,
Александрийским столпом и Пизанской башней,
Стремлением Гольфстрима согреть Северный полюс.

Я люблю тебя буквой закона тяготения
И приговором к смертной казни,
К смертной казни через вечное падение
В твой бездонный Бермудский треугольник.

## Joan Ariete
## Two poems
*Translated from the Kapampangan by Shon Arieh-Lerer and the author*

Joan Ariete is a Filipino poet from Pampanga, who writes in Kapampangan and Tagalog. She has translated a number of contemporary Greek poets into Kapampangan.

### About a boy from a different time

Once upon a time, when the world was flat,
and we ate canteen food every day,
you noticed that I drank with my pinky up.

Once upon a time, when tall boys parted their hair in the
    middle
and delicate girls used baby powder and lip gloss,
you said I looked pretty when I laughed.
My eyes danced
and made your stomach ache.
They enticed your Catholic loins to sin.

Once upon a time, when the world could not see
our brick legs and thorny arms,
you told me that the heart is a storage room
without windows, immune to the mousy girls
who would slit their wrists to walk in my shoes.

Once upon a time, when the thought of not remembering
    your address
was as alien to me as sleeping with a boy I did not love,
you told me that life owes us lemons and chocolate bars
and all the things that Lubao will not give us.
You told me that our ancient wealth
had been stolen,
that our skin is not as white as it should be,
our noses too wide,
our hair too dark, darker than a July typhoon.
Weeks later, as you kissed my hair,
you murmured another girl's name.

Now my eyes don't dance any more.
I see you lying on our waterbed,
dreaming of that ancient wealth.
I see you reaching in the dark for someone
walking in my shoes, the blood drying on her purple wrists.

# Why I left

People ask me
why I left the sweeping green
and brown of my dew-blessed land.
Pampanga, where men get drunk half-naked
and rage at the relentless sun
that burns their hearts,
their wavering resolve.
Where at dawn they wake up to menthol cigarette smoke,
and the crackling laughter
of wives who dye their hair a shameless burgundy.
Where shoeless children play,
dragging calloused feet through puddles of wasted time.

I will not lie.
Leaving Pampanga is a badge I wear,
a row of shining medals on my chest,
a scar on my cheek.

I packed a bagful of clothes
and my dripping pens.

When my country failed me,
I failed it in return,
and loved it even more.

People ask me
why I left the sweeping green
and brown of my dew-blessed land.
I will not lie.
We are a nation of emigrants:
the only truth I have,
and the only truth there is.

# Robert Hull
# A Lancashire Jorge Luis Borges

## Shedding a voice

In my late teens and early twenties my speech, like that of many others who moved from the north of England to the south, shifted from dialect towards something like 'standard'. As a boy I spoke a 'broad' Lancashire dialect, but going to Cambridge – as the first of my family to any university, and somewhat overwhelmed there by the assured tones of the southern public school – I lost much of that first voice and, by a kind of social osmosis presumably, picked up something of another.

Perhaps this socially induced refurbishment of voices happens far less now, but it must have been many people's experience as late as the sixties. It leaves me still with a sense of deprivation, wondering what original spontaneity might have been lost through my speech having taken on at some point an overlay of caution – a mask of speech, the need to speak right – that is perhaps never quite shaken off.

Reading some of Borges' poems in which he reaches to the European far north for inspiration, to the world of the Saxons and their poetry, I was taken by the idea of trying to resurrect that forsaken 'northern' voice – the voice I remember speaking and whose inflections lie at the back of the mind, pressed into service occasionally on comic duty, audible too in moments of stress.

How would it sound, to try to summon back such a voice? Could any of that presumed spontaneity be recovered, in performing translations? Would the elegance of Borges' verse defeat the attempt? 'The original is unfaithful to the translation,' Borges wrote of one criticised translation of his: not a remark ever likely to be turned back on him.

It helps that my faded dialect voice is in some ways a clearly remembered voice. For instance, to mention words from the Borges poems I've tried, I recall 'night' pronounced as 'neet', 'right' as 'reet'. The 'i' of 'light', though, was flat and further back in the mouth, almost a diphthong: 'l(a)ight'. 'Sword' also was nearly a diphthong - 's(w)o-erd'. 'Iron' was 'i-ern', two syllables, the second beginning with a 'y' sound. Spelling them, I've compromised, keeping 'sword', but trying out 'iern'.

The most regular features were the shortening of 'the' to a 't' that was often hardly audible, the dropping 'g' in 'ing' words, and a general loss of 'h' sounds. Grammatically, 'as' was a favourite all-purpose relative pronoun; 'them' and 'her' were often nominatives; and 's' verb endings – as in 'laikes' – were normal in the first person singular and third person plural. 'Tha' ' (for 'thee') was usual. 'Oo' was usual for 'who' and for 'she'. And so on.

But 'clearly remembered' only up to a point. Did we say 'dahn' for 'down' – or 'dehwn', or 'dowen'? 'Abaht' for 'about' – or 'abowt'/ 'abou-ewt'? One reason I'm not sure may be Galapagos-like local variations. I recall standing at the bus stop listening to 13-year-olds from Tarleton, a village three miles from mine, thinking how strange their accent was.

These uncertainties derive also from the decay of dialectal spelling. Familarity with our own (received) speech means native speakers have no trouble with anti-phonetic spellings like 'knight' and 'cough'. Sounding out, as reader, (refreshed) dialect spellings is more precarious.

Here, trying to turn what might have been standard translations of Borges into dialect at least throws up things that might seem useful to the verse-writer. I'm struck by the fact that a continuous elision of articulations that are necessary to the fastidious delivery of standard tends to speed up speech. So, 'He was bitten by the dog' becomes "E were bit bi t'dog' – two stresses not three. The definite article is often an awkward stile for the verse-line to climb; easier that it disappears to a hint of 't'.

So far so good, and in the spirit, perhaps, of Fernando Pessoa's suggestion that 'many poems would gain . . . by being translated into the very language they were written in . . .'

But in general, these versions – given all the elisions – seem rather more laconic than the originals. To instance particular lines, the five stresses of 'La nieve de Northumbria ha conocido/ Y ha olvidado la huella de tus pasos' become the three stresses of 'Northumbria's snows've known / an' forgotten t'prints o' thi feet', with 5 or 6 syllables a line fewer. And so generally.

Compression may not always be a virtue. In fact it might seem like pure loss when we attend to the music of Borges' Spanish. The directness, even simplicity of his verse moves with, and carries with it, river-like almost, a rich, even sumptuous music. It's audible in the beautiful five-stress lines of his sonnets: 'Lento in la lenta sombra labrarias / Metaforas de espadas en los mares'. And in the gathering together of his dynamic lists, as in the list-poem 'Hengist wants men', where the culminating list-coda is thrilling both intellectually and as sound. And in 'Fragmento', the simple repeated 'themes' first of 'Una espada que . . .', then of 'Una espada para la mano' introduce, musically, a dazzling series of syntactic variations and shifts of mini-narrative made the more dramatic by being conducted mainly in substantives.

For all that, maybe the voice of dialect here is to some extent a faithful echo of the dry-ish northern voice I remember, turned away from fuss and elegance and towards a succinct say-it-and-be-done-ness. Maybe it still has its verse uses.

But as for recovering a degree of lost spontaneity, I'm not sure. Perhaps there's ideological fantasy in that idea. And standard certainly now feels easier.

# To a Saxon poet

*(The poet referred to here is the author of 'The Wanderer')*

Northumbria's snow's known
an' forgotten t'prints o' thi feet.
T'suns as've gone dahn between us,
they're not countable, grey brother.
Slowly in slo'-shiftin' shade tha'd fashion thi metaphors
abowt swoerds at sea an' th'orror roamin' t'pines,
an' t'loneliness thi days fetch'd thee.
Whearever's thi face, thi name, to be found now?
Nay, them's things fer 'owd oblivion's keepin'.
'Ow it'll 'ave bin wi' thee then,
when tha wor a man on th'earth,
ah'm never to know now.
Tha went thi ways dahn th'exile's roads.
Now tha's nowt but thi iern song.

# A Un Poeta Sajon

La nieve de Northumbria ha conocido
Y ha olvidado la huella de tus pasos
Y son innumerables los ocasos
Que entre nosotros, gris hermano, han sido,
Lento en la lenta sombra labrarias
Metafores de espadas en los mares
Y del horror que mora en los pinares
Y de la soledad que traen los dias.
Donde buscar tus rasgos y tu nombre?

Esas son cosas que el antiguo olvido
Guarda. Nunca sabre como habra sido
Cuando sobre le tierra fuiste un hombre,
Seguiste los caminos del destierro;
Ahora solo eres tu cantar de hierro.

---------------------------

## To a Saxon poet

*(This Saxon poet is the monk who composed 'The Battle of Brunanburh')*

Thee 'ose flesh,
as is nowt now but dust an' earth-scruff,
once trod its weight on th'earth, same as ours,
thee 'ose eyes took in 't'sun, that grand star,
thee as didn't live in t'rigid clutch o' yesterd'y
but in t'never-endin' present,
on th'igh summit an' dizzyin' tip o' time,
thee as were call'd i' thi monastery te be th'ancient voice of
    epic,
thee as wove words,
thee as sung t'victory o' Brunanburh,
attributin' it not te God
but te t'sword o' t'king,
thee as wi' wild jubilation celebrated swords of iern,
an' t'Vikin's 'umblin',
that feast fer t'raven an' eagle,
thee as marshalled i' thi military ode
thi' tribe's practised metaphors,
thee as in a time without 'ist'ry

saw t'past in t'present
an' in t'blood an' sweat o' Brunnanburh
a mirror wi' old dawns in it,
thee as greatly loved yer England
an' didn' give 'er a name –
today tha're nowt but words
as some Germans scrawls notes on,
today tha're nowt but mi voice
when it brings yer iern words back te bein'.
An' ah'm prayin' te mi gods or te th'ole edifice o' time
that oblivion rewards mi days,
an' like Ulysses ah gets to be called No-man,
an 'ow some verse o' mine'll endure
on neets reet fer rememberin'
or in t'mornin's o' men.


## 'Engist wants men – AD 449


'Engist wants men.
They'll come from t'fringes o' dunes that slip inte great seas,
    from 'uts full o' smoke, from wore-out land, from deep
    forests wi 'wolves, whear in ther vague middle Evil lurks.
Labourers'll leave t'plough and fisherlads ther nets.
They'll leave ther wives an' littl'uns, fer a man reckons 'ow in
    any stretch o'dark 'e can meet one an' make t'other.
'Engist t'mercenary wants men.
'E wants 'em so 'e can take over an island as still isn't called
    England.
They'll follow 'im, bein' weak and cruel.
They know 'e wer always first in t'battles o' men.
They know 'ow e' once forgot 'is duty o'revenge an' 'ow 'e wer
    'anded a naked sword an't'sword did its work.

They'll face up te t'sea wi' ther oars, an' no compass an' no
    mast.
They'll carry swords an' bucklers, 'elmets wi' t'shape o' wild
    boar, spells fer makin' cornfields out e' cornfields, misty
    ideas abaht t'stars an' sun, tales o' Goths an' 'Uns.
They'll conquer t'land, but never go inte t'cities as Rome
    abandoned, because them things is too complicated fer
    t'barbarian mind.
'Engist wants 'em fer victory, fer pillagin', fer corruptin' flesh,
    an' fer oblivion.
'Engist wants 'em ( tho' 'e doesn't know it ) so's t'greatest
    empire's founded, so Shakespeare an' Whitman sings, so
    Nelson's ships rules t'sea, so Adam an' Eve tek ther leave of
    t'Paradise they've lost, 'and in 'and, sayin' nowt.
'Engist wants men ( but 'e won't know it ) so ah can shape
    these letters.


## Hengest Cyning

*T'king's Epitaph*

Under this stone lies t'body of 'Engist –
'as founded i' these islands
first kingdom o' t'royal 'ouse of Odin
an' sated t'greed o' th'eagles.

*T'king speaks*

What runes th' iern'll carve i' t'stone ah don't know –
mi own words is these:
Under th'eavens ah were 'Engist, mercenary.
Ah sold mi courage and stren'th te kings o' lands
o t'sunset, by t' sea call'd Warrior Arm'd Wi' t'Spear',
but stren'th an' courage don't reckon much
on men sellin' 'em,
so after ah'd slash'd t'earth t'foes o' t'British king
reet across 't'North,
I reliev'd 'im o' life an'daylight.
Ah laikes this kingdom as ah seized wi' mi own sword.
It's got rivers fer th'oar an' t'net
an' gradely long summers
an' land fer t'plough an' farms
an' Britons te work 'em
an' cities o'stone we'll present te ruin an' desolation,
because t'dead live there.
Ah' knows 'ow be'ind 'mi back,
t'Britons calls me traitor,
but ah've bin true te mi own courage
an' never trusted mi fate t'other folks' 'ands
an' no man's nerv'd hissel up te betray me.

# Fragment

A sword,
A sword of iern forg'd in t'cold o'dawn,
A sword wi' runes
As none'll leave off thinkin' of and none'll read reet,
A sword from t'Baltic they'll sing abaht in Northumbria,
A sword as poets'll compare
T'ice an' fire,
A sword as a king'll 'and to another king
An' 'im to a dream,
A sword as'll be true
Te th'ower as Destiny already knows abaht,
A sword as'll light up t'battlefield.

A sword fer th'and
That'll rule t'grand battle, men's weavin',
A sword fer th'and
That'll stain red t'wolf's fangs
An' t'pitiless beak o' t'corbie,
A sword fer th'and
That'll scatter round t'red gowd,
A sword fer th'and
That'll bring death te t'snake in 'er den o' gowd ,
A sword fer th'and
That'll win a kingdom and lawse a kingdom,
A sword fer th'and
That'll bring down t'forest o' spears.
A sword te fit th'and o' yon Beowulf.

# Itzik Manger's 'Amon un Tamar' and Heinrich Heine's 'Die Liebe begann im Monat März . . .'
## *Translated by Murray Citron*

Itzik Manger was born in Rumania in 1900. He lived in Warsaw in the 1930's. In 1938 he moved to Paris. He escaped to Marseilles before the Germans came, and made his way to North Africa, and then to England. After the war he moved to New York. Then he moved to Israel. He died there in 1968.

Manger's work is entirely in Yiddish. The poem 'Amnon un Tamar' is based on 2 Samuel 13. It is part of a series in which Manger reworked the King David epic. The Yiddish original is found in Manger's collection, *Medresh Itzik* (Jerusalem, 1969). The transliteration to Latin alphabet is based on the Yivo system.

The third stanza of Manger's poem refers to 'Heine's poem'. There are likely other Heine lyrics with a nightingale and spring flowers, but this one fits. The rhyme scheme in the German original is AABB. March and heart don't rhyme in English. The translation settles on ABCB.

Manger was much influenced by Heine. They share a quality of precision in versification and word choice. Both were romantic balladeers, and satirists. With both it is often hard to tell where sentiment leaves off and irony begins. Hemingway's General Golz can speak for them: 'We are very serious so we can make very strong jokes.'

## Amnon and Tamar

I write you this letter, Tamar, to take care,
So far we haven't been caught.
Keep the secret, first, from our father the king,
And if you can, from God.

Do you remember that night in the wood,
When I called you, 'wife'?
You trembled and said, 'Let me go, let me go,'
And I said, 'Stay, it's for life!'

You stayed. And just like in Heine's poem,
The nightingale sang of spring,
And cherry trees scattered over us
Their early blossoming.

And I was ecstatic: 'Tamar, do you hear
How my body is calling to you?'
And you gave your answer heavy and hot,
'Amnon, I do, I do.'

And drunk with 'the one' and with 'you alone',
I knew you and your charms,
And carried you round and round in the wood,
Naked in my arms.

And the wood was astonished. 'Oh my, oh my,
What message does this send?'
No Jewish forest its whole life long
Ever saw such an event.

And then suddenly in a thin high wail
You cried for the night to end,
And the ancient Talmudic brain of the wood
Began to comprehend.

.Your cry was a menace, it frightened the wood,
And it made me since that night
Abhor the wood. Why did you scream,
And not sing and laugh with delight?

I remind you again, Tamar, take care,
Make sure we don't get caught.
Keep the secret, first, from Daddy-O,
And if you can, from God.


## Amnon un Tamar


Ikh shrayb dir dos brivl, Tamar,
To ze hit op dem sod,
Der eykrshrt farn tateshi,
Un oyb du kenst, far Got.

Gedenkst di nakht in vildn vald,
Ven kh'hob dikh gerufn 'Vayb'?
Du host gefivert: 'Loz mikh geyn!'
Un ikh hob geheysn, 'Blayb!'

Un du bist geblibn. Di nakhtigal
Hot, punkt vi in Haynes lid
Opgetrayselt iber uns
Dem ershtn karshenblit.

Un ikh hob gefivert: 'Tamar, du herst
Vi s'zingt tsu dir mayn guf?'
Un du host geotemt hays un shver:
'Ikh entfer oyf dayn ruf.'

Un shikur fun 'shayn', fun 'mit dir aleyn'
Hob ikh dikh dort derkent
Un kh'hob dikh a nakete durkhn vald
Getrogn oyf mayne hent.

Un der vald hot geshtoynt: 'U-ma, u-ma,
Vi azoy iz dos geshen?'
A Yidisher vald hot zint er lebt
Aza zeung nisht gezen.

Nor ven du host plutzem aroysgeplatst
Mit a sharf un din geveyn
Hot der alter Talmudisher kop fun vald
Ersht ongehoybn farshteyn.

Dayn geveyn hot gemusert, mayd oys dem vald,
Vi ikh mayd im zint yener nakht;
O, far vos hostu demolt geveynt in vald
Un nisht gezungen, geshtift un gelakht?

Ikh shrayb dir dos brivl, Tamar,
To ze hit op dem sod,
Der eykrsht farn tateshi,
Un oyb du kenst, far Got.

# Heinrich Heine, 'Die Liebe begann im Monat Mai . . .'

Die Liebe begann im Monat März,
Wo mir erkrankte Sinn und Herz.
Doch als der Mai, der grüne, kam:
Ein Ende all mein Trauern nahm.

Es war am Nachmittag um Drei
Wohl auf der Moosbank der Einsiedelei,
Die hinter der Linde liegt versteckt,
Da hab ich ihr mein Herz entdeckt.

Die Blumen dufteten. Im Baum
Die Nachtigall sang, doch hörten wir kaum
Ein einziges Wort von ihrem Gesinge,
Wir hatten zu reden viel wichtige Dinge.

Wir schwuren uns Treue bis in den Tod.
Die Stunden schwanden, das Abendrot
Erlosch. Doch sassen wir lange Zeit
Und weinten in der Dunkelheit.


Love began in the month of March,
My mind and heart were weak and ill.
Then came the warm green month of May,
My mind and heart were hale and well.

At three o'clock in the afternoon,
Behind the linden where breezes stir,
On a mossy bank at the hermitage
I spoke and opened my heart to her.

The flowers were sweet. The nightingale
Sang in the tree, and we scarcely heard
A single word of his warbling.
We shared what in two hearts was stored.

We swore to be true to each other till death.
The hours went by. The crimson sun
Went down. We sat for long and wept
For what will come and will be gone.

# Valéry Larbaud
## 'Scenes'
### *Translated by Padraig Rooney*

Valéry Larbaud, born in 1881, was heir to a Vichy mineral water fortune which allowed him to lead the high life around Europe's capitals and spas. His peripatetic, dandyish persona is embodied in the fictitious Barnabooth who narrates much of the poetry. Translator of Whitman and overseer of Joyce translations, Larbaud was fluent in six languages. His poetry is cosmopolitan, making use of masks, voices, nostalgia and eroticism in a way that recalls the great moderns: Pessoa, Eliot and Joyce. He died in 1957.

# Scenes

1

Once, in a working-class area of Kharkov,
in that Russian south of white-shawled women
carrying themselves like Madonnas, I spotted
a young woman coming back from the well
balancing two buckets on the ends of a pole
across her neck and shoulders. (As they've done
in those parts since Ovid's day.)
                                        And I saw
a child in rags go up and speak to her.
She inclined sideways – gently, dexterously –
so as to lower the bucket of spring water
to the ground, level with the child's lips.
He got down on his knees to drink his fill.

2

One morning, in Rotterdam, on the Boompjes Quay
(around 8 o' clock, September 18, 1900)
I spotted two factory girls on their way to work.
Opposite one of the great railway bridges
they said their goodbyes, went separate ways,
kissing sweetly, their trembling hands wanting
and not wanting to part. Their mouths sadly
touched and went, touched again, eyes staring
fixedly into the other's eyes ...
                                        In this way
they spent a last long minute close together,
standing in the way of the busy passers-by,
while tugs hooted on the river, trains whistled
and shunted on the bridge.

**3**

Between Cordoba and Seville, a small station
where the Southern Express always stops
for no apparent reason. In vain you might
look past this sleepy station for a village
under the eucalyptus trees. All you'll see is
the green and gold Andalusian countryside.
Opposite, on the far side of the tracks,
sits a hut of blackened branches and earth.
At the sound of your train a knot of ragged kids
comes from the hut to the edge of the platform.
Leading them, the eldest girl, silent, smiling,
dances for coins, her feet blackened by dirt,
her dark face dirty and without charm.
Through the rips of her ash-coloured skirt
you can see her naked, jiggling, skinny thighs,
her wrinkled little yellow belly. She dances,
dances for you, and for the gentlemen laughing
in the restaurant wagon, in the smell of cigars.

# Eugene Dubnov
# Two poems
*Translated by Anne Stevenson with the author*

## It was in Riga in the yard . . .

It was in Riga, in the yard:
how you jumped, a boy, into a snowdrift,
and on the high icy hill
launched your sledge. In Tallinn,

the wardrobe on the right and stove
where branches hung down outside the window
and in the other room
you cried – Father had punished you.

And when Mummy called from the window
summoning you back indoors
you pressed against the house: the wall
was cold and clammy.

In sunlit Tashkent where what's left of us
is a grave, how you yelled
when, to make you walk faster, your brother
painfully squeezed your neck.

The air, the breeze in your earliest backyard,
a spring evening, the ships,
the school, the stresses of difficult words,
Grandfather and 'Behave yourself, boy!'

Every time, on finishing his stewed prunes,
He'd say: 'That was good'
and slowly wipe his mouth with a napkin.
One day he went away and didn't come back.

And deeper yet, without being afraid of
the dark cellar, you'll go in,
come out and see the clothesline
by a fence in summer, and you'll find

a pen-knife there and see yourself
rushing eagerly on a balmy day
along Graniidi street, crying 'Daddy!' –
and the sunset was fire.

Did it or didn't it happen? In winter
the springy soft feel of running in felt boots,
skating on ice, and impossible to keep
your hands behind your back, and flakes

falling on the rink, as later on Moscow's
music and din – but not a soul
there on the lake where the sound
was only of skates and the snow

rustling in the trees . . . and how whenever
you played 'knocker-out' in a grassy field
you couldn't throw the ball far enough. How
the morning star rose over the school-leavers dance.

To whom did this all happen, how long ago –
the winds, the smell of the sea, the sky?
It hurts, there's no return;
once again, your head is spinning.

But why resurrect that long-gone world,
drag it into the light,
make an icon of the past,
turn the pages of yellowing years?

Why strain to revive yet again
the first three-storey apartment block,
the room, the wide bed
where you lay between Mummy and Father?

Why once more walk slowly home
along the sleeping streets
from the death-delivering telegraph-office
through the empty, echoing town? What's

all this – a lie, or a death mask, or a muscle
where hot blood beats?
Life will not tell. The answer perhaps
will come in the wake of the promise.

## Parents

Where were they looking, what did they see
behind the camera when it snatched this snapshot?
Were there winter bursts of gold acacia seed,
dazzling fields of glassy summer frost?
Neither music nor language can translate
that captured instant into sounds now.
Every word they said or note they sang
has gone forever into exile. Here,
on this side of time's lens, a V of geese is flying,
and at my feet a fine young tuberous onion
is growing warm enough to melt the spring snow.

# Grete Tartler
# Two poems
*Translated by Adam Sorkin*

Grete Tartler has published nine collections of poetry and six volumes of essays. Starting in 1992, she served Romania as a diplomat in Vienna, Copenhagen, Reykjavik, and Athens. Tartler has translated from German, Arabic, English, and Danish, and she has written on Arab poetry and culture.

## Qasida

*Mikarrin mifarrin muqbilin mudbi'in ma'an*
this is what I recite for the galloping horse.
The blood moistens the desert, the consonants.
The yolk of the earth separates from the sky.
The temple, an abandoned arena.
Left behind, the sacrificial knife
and on its blade a gleam
      on the sky golden mouths
      on the palate of the golden mouths
      other golden mouths.

All keep summoning me.

## Siddartha

Poetry sometimes is murky, pointless,
other times restless like a breeze –
try to follow the middle way, a perfectly tuned violin
neither absorbed into the world nor alone.
Stelian is telling us that during World War I
airplanes' wings had wires that needed to be rigged
to the same precise tension.
Not having the proper apparatus,
the Romanians summoned a violinist.
The planes all flew, some successfully, others in vain.
But what of the violinist?
Nobody knew his name.
Maybe he died under the bombs, under the apple tree
that burst into bloom while he was tuning.

# Bohdan Ihor Antonych
# Two poems
*Translated by Steve Komarnyckyj*

Bohdan Ihor Antonych (1909–37) took the folklore language and traditions of the Lemke region, which was part of Poland between the first and second world wars, and transplanted them into literary Ukrainian. The Lemke were a Ukrainian mountain people whose culture and traditions were rooted in crop cycles and pagan mythology and, in Antonych's work, the boundaries between the narrator, the natural world and the music of the poems become blurred within an ecstatic pagan celebration of life.

The ethnic community in which Antonych's language was rooted was destroyed after the war when, during a brutal exercise termed 'Operation Vistula', the Lemke were deported from their homeland in order to crush the Ukrainian underground and resettled elsewhere in Poland (http://en.wikipedia.org/wiki/Operation_Vistula#Deportations_and_repressions). There is still an active Lemke Ukrainian community but the organic connection to the soil has been broken and the variant of Ukrainian spoken by Antonych only exists like a specimen preserved in formaldehyde.

# Duet

We return slowly to the earth, our cradle.
Green tangles of vegetation bind us, two fettered chords.
The razor sharp axe of sun hews at a trunk,
The music of moss, tenderness of the breeze, the oak a proud
    idol.

In the wastage of days that bear us, the body, warm and
    obedient
Grows with itself, two siblings two flowers of fidelity.
The moss warms us like cat fur. You transform the stars into
    a murmur
And blood into music and greenery. The sky glows.

At the edge of day, in the ocean of heaven, the winds of the
    future sleep
And our devoted constellations wait under the frost,
While earth does not instruct them to arise. We abandon
    things,
To be borne, to grasp the stars in pure ecstasy.

The yearning of blood hurts. Eyebrows sharp as two arrows,
While above us a wall of melody echoes
The pinions of a breeze. Our fate pinned on the planets.
You burn with growth, thirsty as the earth. Become all
    music.

# Idolatrous nights

The refraction of the moon repeats itself in the clouds, a song,
Cloud on cloud forming a silver wall, below which the foxes
    bark.
Leaves dangle from the stars in oblique ropes,
The mushrooms chime their plates of rust colour,
In the forest choir,

The leaves of the oak form
A lush foam, a surf, that booms and trumpets
The unwritten law of night.
Wolves bring their sacrifice of blood and flesh
Wiping their muzzles on musical flax.

Night of predatory law and dark magic. In the marsh things
    knead
A dull red dough of mud. Owls harmonise treason.
A star wrinkles its eyebrow at the moon,
Flower sticks to flower,
In a dew thick as paste,

The oily greenery
Becomes this coarse fabric of darkness.
The angles of roots are coiled music, plaiting
The melodies that foam within.
This is the heart of the forest,

The horizon's secret,
Where storms exhaust themselves and lightning
Is a razor whipped across a razor,
Each broken human dream.
Its wings sweep across the earth, adorning roofs

With wreaths for the marriage of fire.
Terror, a subterranean child that cries each night
In that place where beyond knowledge of feeling or ruin
The incomprehensible, ancient speech surrounds us.
The river. Spring grinds its ice.

Paul Celan
Two poems
*Translated by Alfred Corn*

## This evening also (Auch heute abend)

Denser –
Now that snow has also fallen on this
Sea awash with sunlight –
Ice flowers in the hampers
You're carrying to town.

Sand's
What you ask in exchange,
Given that the last
Rose left back home
Wants, this evening also, to be fed
With an hour's light snow.

## One eye, opened (Ein Auge, offen)

Hours, May-tinted, cool.
What's no longer to be named, hot,
audible in your mouth.

Nobody's voice, back again.

Stinging, deep, apple of the eye:
your eyelid
doesn't block the path, nor lashes
record what enters.

A tear (halved),
a sharper lens (portable),
restores the pictures for you.

# Poems by Wiliguru Pambardu and Parraruru
## Translated from the Yindjibarndi by Shon Arieh-Lerer

The Yindjibarndi poets Pambardu and Parraruru are considered
the foremost twentieth-century bards of the Western Australian
Pilbara desert, composing their works during a time when the
people of the Pilbara were first coming into contact with Western
civilization.

The blind poet Pambardu, who died in 1934, lived at a time
when his culture faced momentous changes that had made its
tradition fragile. His poetry is a vivid record of these changes.
Many of Pambardu's poems, including 'Desert Life', are awestruck
and fascinated reactions to the first machinery ever seen by the
Yindjibarndi people.

Parraruru, though of the Ngarluma people, was one of the
most prolific Yindjibarndi language poets and storytellers of
the second half of the twentieth-century. He was a *mawarnkarra*
(magician) who was believed to possess remarkable powers. He
worked extensively with linguists and anthropologists, who
recorded his Yindjibarndi and Ngarluma oral literature and
descriptions of life in the Pilbara desert.

## *Wiliguru Pambardu*

# Desert Life

At the spout of the pump lies a trough,
at the spout of the pump a dead man rises.
Early dawn, with metal clanging,
the dead man wanders through the windmill's shadow.

The pumping rod screeches.
The tail turns, clangs,
casts shadows.

Its iron innards stir, turning the pumping, coughing wheel.
Who sits in its shining heart, driving the rod into the
    ground?

## *Parraruru*

# How I make spears

I broke a branch off a tree
and thinned it down
and made a barb
and fitted the barb onto the branch.
I smoothed it.
I straightened it.
I heated it in the ashes.
I went and had a fight.

The tip pierced straight through the man.
I pulled it out
and with it came some flesh.
The man fell down.
Because I had stabbed him, he let urine.
'I can't get up.'
Because I had stabbed him, he stayed lame for good.

## *Parraruru*

# Change

A foreigner came to our land and ate its forbidden food. Our
land sent a whirlwind, gusting, powerful, picking up pebbles,
stones, cutting down trees, whirling them and throwing
them into the waters.

The snake of the waters was angered.
Our camp was unprotected by magic.

The magician of our people came back from his hunt.
'Spear the snake, slash it, kill it,' we told him.

The wind spun sand through our camp, covered us in stones,
and slung water into the air. The magician hurled his magic
crystal through the water, and the water fell to the ground
and slithered back into its crater.

This is all I can tell you.

## *Parraruru*

## Stranger

A man comes from another land and brings with him foreign
    magic.
He calls our men into the desert.
We sit in a circle. He throws the magic into the middle.
He unwraps it and tells us, 'Here is my magic.'
'Who do you want to kill?' we ask.
He points. 'I want to kill that man.'
One of us stands up. 'No, don't kill him. I like that man.
I think he should live. Why do you want to kill him? What
    did he do to you?'
'He sent this magic after me, now I will send it after him.'
'Where did the magic go when he sent it?'
'It went west, toward my land.'
'We did not see it.'
More of us stand up. 'We did not see it.
We have never seen magic sent to the west.
This man has not killed anyone, and we like him.
He is a harmless and quiet man.
Since time began, we have never seen your magic in our land.
This magic is from another land, not from ours.
We want this man to live.
Do not do anything to him. Do not kill him.
Do not make the magic speak.
Do not make the magic enter his stomach.
Your magic will blight us. It must not speak.'
We seize the magic. We smash it,
and burn it.

# Sasha Dugdale
# William Blake in Russia

We translated Blake's *Songs of Innocence and of Experience* in March, on the outskirts of a town called Korolev, just outside Moscow. Spring was late, it was minus eighteen and the back roads were compacted snow, the pavements were hidden by mountainous drifts. I only saw Korolev by night, the blocks of housing set back from the road, a white park filled with black leafless trees, a few people at a bus stop, women in coloured sheepskins and hats hurrying across the road. A monument in the park wore a wedge of white on its bowed granite head and shoulders. We passed a long fence made of cement panels, and behind it a factory.

The factory makes space rockets to be sent into orbit from Baikonur, and the town itself served the Soviet space programme and bears the name of its chief engineer, Sergei Korolev. Korolev is the thickset black statue wearing a crown of snow, immortalised Soviet-fashion, stepping forward into the unknown. Even at the time it struck me as odd that we should be translating the poet Blake in such proximity to a town dedicated to the conquering of space by mathematical order.

Blake, the visionary, writes of the scientific perception of the sun as a ball of fire: 'O no,no, I see an Innumerable company of the Heavenly host crying, "Holy, Holy, Holy is the Lord God Almighty."' Korolev, at a discussion on space landing craft, writes on a piece of paper: 'The moon is hard.'

Blake has been translated into Russian before. There are classic translations of Blake from the beginning of the century, but I have been asked to work with a group of translators on a new and complete translation of the *Songs* to be published in Russian alongside the illustrated plates. Marina Boroditskaia and Grigorii Kruzhkov, both translators and poets themselves, lead the seminar and my role is to introduce Blake and then to comment on the accuracy of the translations, their consonance with the English, whilst Marina and Grigorii comment on their poetic merit. The translators, mostly professional translators, with whom I have already worked on an anthology of contemporary British poetry, work in the afternoons on poems from the *Songs* which they have chosen. There is a loose agreement that the translators will pick different poems unless they feel particularly drawn to a poem. If two translations are successful then they will both be published as variations on a theme. There is no tradition of literal translation of poetry in Russia. The translations will be judged as poems in their own right.

There is no doubt that the enterprise will succeed, for as Blake wrote: 'If the Sun & Moon should doubt / Theyd immediately Go out.' Still the task is quite unusually momentous, both in dimension and difficulty. The forty-five poems of the *Songs of Innocence and of Experience* are just that: songs, and they must retain their lyricism and their eccentricities in Russian. They must sound simple and naive, child-like and yet heightened. Gilchrist writes of them:

> . . . the effect was as that of an angelic voice singing to oaten pipe, such as Arcadians tell of; or, as if a spiritual magician were summoning before human eyes, and through a human medium, images and scenes of divine loveliness . . .

If this natural, lyrical and apparently divine spontaneity is not conveyed in Russian then the project will have been a failure. Moreover the peculiar world of Blake must be brought into Russian. There are no spiritual equivalents. Blake was self-taught and independent, he stood at odds to tradition and school, and his writing and his art were spiritual acts. As he stood alone in English, so he must sound like no one else in translation.

On the first morning I give a short biographical introduction to Blake. I describe Blake's childhood, the London dissenter household, his schooling at home, the visions he sees. I describe his technical skills as an engraver and the technique he invented for making his own books. The group listens politely, but they are clearly desperate to be working. Marina begins apportioning the poems in an amusingly girls' school manner: 'Which sweep are you taking? Innocent or Experienced?' 'Who's got the sick rose?' 'Can anyone be an ancient bard by tomorrow?' The lack of reverence and boundless appetite for translation is disarming: it suggests that there is nothing sacred or secret about poetry translation – it is an honest craft, best practised rather than discussed. Highly trained honest craftsmen may lend themselves to an ancient bard, as to a sick rose. This approach finds its parallel in Blake's own poetry. We are too used to presenting it as a work of wild inspiration: the books of *Songs of Innocence and of Experience* in fact took many hours of painstaking work with dangerous acids and varnishes to create, and the resulting plates were the work of a husband and wife team, rather than a single artistic genius. I can hear industrious Catherine Blake saying, 'Mr Blake, will you hand me the Innocent Sweep for colouring?'

We meet every morning and listen to the completed translations. The translator reads the poem and we follow the text on a projector. Then the group members comment. I cannot imagine this happening in England: they respond with honesty, sometimes admiration, sometimes disgust. The openness is refreshing, but also hard to bear. At times I see some very crestfallen faces.

Russian translation practice is very different from British. I have done several translation workshops in Russia in which translators have worked together, or commented and made suggestions about the work of others. I believe British poetry translators to be less inclined to allow others to fine-tune their poetic output.

I often wonder whether I would have survived Russian-style intervention and advice to have any sort of individual voice. But looking at my highly vocal and highly original Russian friends and colleagues, I suspect the process has strengthened them in their own convictions.

On the other hand Russian translators have no sense of being the handmaidens of literature. Grigorii often tells me that the translator is in competition with the poet – who can woo the poem with the greatest success? Poetry translations must be poems in their own right in Russia, they must be at least as great as the original, and greater, if possible. A British translator might strive to keep close to the wording of an original poem, but a Russian translator would put the spirit and feel of a poem first, and would substitute detail where necessary. A British translator might aim to produce a text which did not belong in the British experience, a strange voice from outside. A Russian translator would aim to produce a poem which sat so well in the national psyche it came to be seen as a Russian poem. I am generalising: translation is a broad church. However these trends are particularly marked in my experience, and who is to say which approach is better? Still it would be fair to note that many Russians read and know literature in translation and can quote at length from Burns and Byron, Kipling and Coleridge. How many people can quote from German, French, Spanish or Russian literature in English translation?

Translation in Russia has a long and honourable tradition. In the repressive atmospheres of both the nineteenth and twentieth centuries it was a way of reaching out to both West and East and escaping cultural isolation. In the twentieth century it was a lifeline for poets such as Akhmatova and Pasternak, who were unable to publish their own work freely. Translated literature informs Russian literature to an extreme degree, from Russia's best known poem, Pushkin's *Eugene Onegin* which takes its cue from Byron, to Pasternak's famous poem 'Hamlet'. Not since Keats looked into Chapman's Homer has translation had such a loud effect here as it constantly has in Russia.

As a result the translator is a prized creature in Russia, and the craft of translation is more widely understood. It is expected, for example, that a translator will be proficient in metre and rhyme. Russian poetry itself is far more formal: even now the majority of poets writing in Russian use full rhyme and their poems are highly metrical in structure. I have a conversation about the decline of poetry in the West into free verse with practically every Russian poet I meet. Russian poets are often quietly depressed about the English translations of their poetry into unrhymed free verse. They want to hear their own poems' lyrical sound and shape in English and they are often far less worried about exact translations of meaning.

All the translations of Blake are fully rhymed, often more fully rhymed than Blake himself, and they observe metre. The metrical difficulty with Blake is that sometimes he moves between metres, and sometimes his metrical patterns are ambiguous or uneven. This helps create a sense of child-like speech and rough spontaneity. It also gives Blake a mobility of expression: take for example the poem 'The Tyger' which opens so famously with the trochaic line 'Tyger Tyger, burning bright' and keeps its trochaic hammer beat for several stanzas whilst describing the blacksmith god that wrought the beast. Blake's poem then pans out to reveal the skies and moves to a more metrically ambiguous line: 'When the stars threw down their spears' – possible to read as trochees, but more naturally as iambs with a trochaic opening. This shift in metre slows the poem down and allows for a brief passage of homage and reflection.

Russian translation practice does not appear to permit this. The group scrutinise the translation of 'The Tyger' and agree collectively that it should remain trochaic throughout, or risk appearing a poor and unskilled translation.

They are also extremely concerned about Blake's visual rhymes: 'eye' and 'symmetry', for example, and question me on such matters. Can I see any situation in which 'symmetry' would rhyme precisely with 'eye'? On this matter Marina is firm. Whether words rhyme precisely or not in English they should be full rhymes in Russian. A further trap lies in the existence of several well-known translations of Blake in Russian: these new translations cannot even inadvertently echo the established translations. Marina, who is tempted to translate Blake's 'The Fly', is quite beside herself with annoyance: whatever she does, however she twists and turns the line she cannot escape the spiderweb of existing rhymes.

But however strict the rules on composition, there is no sense that the wording or the images should be translated exactly. They should be consonant, they should not stand out as inventions, but they need not slavishly adhere to the English. Mostly we agree here: our common sense of literary taste seems to fit, and there is something very reassuring in this fact: whatever the differences of approach, when we are faced with a single translation we all recognise the same qualities of exuberance and truth. Blake's poems of social discontent 'LONDON', 'Holy Thursday', and 'The Chimney Sweeper' seem to me particularly fine in Russian, the freedom to change images giving new poetry in Russia.

The exception is 'The Sick Rose' poem, taken on by a woman who is a fine poet-translator, but whose gift lies in her ability to take a poem and make it hers. This is acceptable Russian translation practice, however her version of Blake's 'The Sick Rose' wrenches the imagery and the meaning of the poem into a different world, and to my ears one which is alien to Blake. There is some debate, but we agree that it will not do. This is a great relief to me. I am able to make notes at our discussion that a poem has departed from the meaning of the original (often feeling stupidly pedantic as I do so), but I am not able to comment on the poetic quality of the translation, and this is far and away the most important consideration in Russia. In another seminar the same poet translated a contemporary British poem into an entirely different poem – different in tone, shape, imagery, argument, but the Russian poem was good, and it was decided that it would be published as a translation. The translator-poet argued to me that the writer of the original would prefer to be represented by a beautiful poem than a dull translation. This did not happen to Blake's 'Rose' and I was gladder than I could say.

For a week we pored over each of the poems, I attempted to describe the force of allegories, so the Russian could hold the allegorical balance with the same sureness, and we wrestled with phrases that were unclear to me in the English. In the 'Garden of Love' I wrestled with my own irritation that there were no true words for the sweet briar in Russian, and then a greater childish irritation when it seemed to me that a poem in Russian was a million mental miles away from Blake, not because of the translator, but because of the language, which made the undoubtedly right words sound like hideous approximations. These moments of translator-rage are like the isolated moments in a loving relationship when you find yourself mad with hate at the loved one's obtuse otherness. And then there are the other moments when a translation is so sweet – Russian exceeds in its natural possibilities, offers such tantalising visions of what Blake might have done had he written in Russian, that English feels like a dead wooden thing, incapable of singing.

After a week most of the poems have been translated and a good number are in their final draft: a feat of translation. On the last evening everyone goes outside to make a snowman in the deep snow and Marina, with her faultless judgement, sniffs the air and says she smells the spring. The next morning the sudden warmth is palpable as we wheel our bags out, and the icicles attempt to loosen themselves from the eaves. The deep drifts are transparent water under a thin crust and Korolev, as we drive through and out, looks desperate beyond words – the rocket factory has an abandoned air about it. It is the sort of day on which even the round earth, let alone the moon, is not hard but a mass of slush and icy standing water. No lunar landings today, and no poetry either. We make our way back to Moscow in the grim wet – minibuses of miserable Blakean angels fallen from paradise.

The Blake seminar was organised and funded by the British Council, who are the joint organisers of a major William Blake exhibition in Russia. My thanks to Rosemary Hilhorst and Anna Genina for their involvement.

# Pushkin
## From *Yevgeni Onegin*
### *Translated by D. M. Thomas*

No literary work I know gives one such a sense of the full
personality of the author as does *Onegin*. Its unique stanza form
– fourteen lines of intricately rhymed tetrameters, with almost as
many feminine line endings as masculine – makes it formidably
hard to translate. As feminine rhymes are much more readily
available in Russian, the 'same' stanza form in English sounds
different, heavier, more deliberately willed, than the Russian.
There are bound to be times when finding perfect rhymes is going
to distract from what Pushkin is saying, and not fully reflect the
original's emotional tone. Likewise there is a temptation to pad
out a tetrameter – which is fatal. On the other hand, a prose
version, such as Nabokov's, is simply not *Onegin*.

My attempted solution has been to tone down the rhymes, free
them up somewhat, by using a lot of half-rhymes, assonance and
enjambement. If there was a conflict between being faithful to
the letter, and faithful to the spirit, I have preferred the spirit.
The months I spent attempting it were extraordinarily happy
ones; a bit like a love affair. For I love Pushkin, and the act of
translation is a wonderful form of intimacy.

# (Chapter Eight)

XXXIX
Days rushed; in the air warming slowly
Winter resolved to be resigned;
And he did not become a poet,
Did not die, did not lose his mind.
The spring enlivens him; his chambers,
Where for so long he's hibernated
Like a ground hog or a woodchuck
– Its double doors and inglenook—
He first leaves on a fine clear morning,
Along the Neva flies his sleigh.
On the blue ice-blocks hacked away
From Neva the sun plays; the thawing
Furrows of snow are churned to mud:
To where, then, does his sleigh, his blood,

XL
Direct Onegin? Yes, exactly!
You've guessed the mission he is on:
The sleigh at pace to his Tatiana
Is bearing my rash hooligan.
Soon, looking like a corpse, he enters
The first hall . . . not a soul . . . He ventures
Further: still no one . . . One room more?
He can't turn back now; when this door
He opens, what can cause Yevgeni
To reel back, shaken? The princess,
Alone, pale, in untidy dress,
Is sitting there, reading a letter,
Her sad face tilted, resting on
Her hand, and her tears streaming down.

## XLI

Who would a deep but silent anguish
In that swift instant not have read?
Who would not know that poor young Tanya
Larina's tears were being shed?
He falls before her, in the madness
Of his regret, remorse, compassion;
She starts, but holds him with her eyes,
In silence and without surprise,
And without anger . . . Just intently
Takes in his sick look, like a light
Put out, his pleading eyes, his mute
Reproach – she takes in all. The tender
And simple girl of former days
Is resurrected, newly raised.

## XLII

For a long time there's only silence.
She does not make Onegin stand;
Allows, as though not realising,
His thirsty lips against her hand . . .
To what dreams has she now surrendered?
It seems the silence will not end, but
Tanya says quietly at last:
'Enough; please get up now. I must
Explain myself to you sincerely.
Onegin, do you recall the time
When in the garden of my home
I listened humbly as so clearly
You spoke the lesson I should learn?
Well, now today it is my turn.

XLIII
In those days I was younger; maybe
A little better-looking too,
And loved you; yet I found, Onegin,
What? – what did I find in you,
In your heart? Nothing but correctness,
Isn't that true? And you expected
Young, humble girls to fall in love
With you. My God! I feel my blood
Freezing today to think how coldly
You looked, and preached at me . . . But I
Don't blame you: in that dreadful time
You acted really rather nobly,
For what you said to me was right;
I thank you now with all my heart.

XLIV
In those days, living in the wilds, far
From rumour, from society
– Isn't this true? – you didn't like me . . .
Why now are you pursuing me?
Why do you make me now your aim, your
Object? . . . Isn't it, Onegin,
Because I am – I have to be –
A part of the nobility?
And then, my husband, maimed in battle,
Is liked and favoured by the court;
Isn't it true, my disrepute
Would bring on us enormous scandal?
Wouldn't that suit you? You'd be sure
To gain a scurrilous allure.

XLV

I'm crying... If indeed your Tanya
You've not forgotten yet, know this:
Your sharp rebuke, your caustic manner,
Your icy-cold, severe discourse,
Could I re-live those past events, I
Would much prefer to this offensive
Passion, these letters and these tears.
You had respect then for my years,
At least showed you were sympathetic
To dreams a young girl may create . . .
But now! – this falling at my feet,
It's shameful, don't you think? Pathetic!
How could you let a trivial
Feeling enslave your heart and soul?

XLVI

To me, Onegin, this existence
Is loathsome. All the luxury,
My triumphs in this tinsel brilliance,
The vortex of society,
My fashionable home, and evenings
– What are they? Masquerades! Believe me,
I'd give it all up for a shelf
Of books, a garden to myself,
Full of wild flowers, and for the places
Where I saw you for the first time,
Onegin; and I even pine
For that poor, silent, humble graveyard,
Where now my dear old nurse is laid
Beneath a cross and branches' shade.

XLVII

Yet happiness was so *possible* . . .
So *close*! . . . But now my fate
Is fixed. I think I was not fully...
Mindful . . . until it seemed too late.
Everyone urged it, mama pleaded,
Her tears kept falling, and for *me* I
Felt that all lots would be the same . . .
And so I married. Now it's time,
You have to leave me now, I beg you;
I know that in your heart reside
A true nobility and pride.
I love you (why should I dissemble?),
But I am someone else's wife;
I shall be true to him all my life.'

XLVIII

She leaves the room. And for Yevgeni,
Who stands in shock, it is as though
A frightful tempest of sensations
Is concentrating blow on blow
Upon his heart! But of a sudden,
A clink of spurs, it's Tanya's husband
Coming; and at this moment when
Our hero's life goes ill, my friends,
I fear that we shall have to leave him,
For a long time . . . for ever. We
Have followed his path faithfully
Quite long enough, don't you agree? It's
The shore at last, thank God. Hooray!
I thought we'd never see the day.

# Denisa Comănescu
## 'Return from Exile'
### *Translated by Adam Sorkin*

Denisa Comănescu has published five books of poetry, among them *Banishment from Paradise* (1979, the winner of a Writers' Union Debut prize), *Boat on the Waves* (1987), and *Now the Biography of Then* in 2000. She currently co-ordinates a world literature series for Humanitas Publishing House.

# Return from Exile

Eleven years, four months and seventeen days.
A short exile?
This notebook isn't the same as then.
I've filled quite a number.
Some were large, bound between gilt covers,
others small, light, made of Bible paper.
At night I touched them in secret,
fingered their membrane-like pages,
each time more urgently, with such
insistent, insatiable desire.
During the day, I didn't dare go near them.
They might as well have been a stranger's.
Later I gave them to friends:
For you, for your new book of poems, I'd tell them.
This brought luck to some, or so they'd pretend.

Then you arrived,
after eleven years, four months and seventeen days.
In the morning, fearless in the light that seems to banish
    death,
we fill membrane after membrane, simply and naturally.
When I turn a page covered with writing,
Orpheus averts his eyes.

# Lowri Gwilym
## 'Returning'
### *Translated by Damian Walford Davies*

Lowri Gwilym, who died suddenly in July 2010 at the age of 55, was a woman in the midst of a life full of purpose and meaning. An award-winning editor for factual programmes at the Welsh-language channel S4C, and before that for the BBC, she travelled between Cardiff and her home village of Trefenter, near Aberystwyth, where she lived with her partner and their two boys. The village was her centre, the place of childhood summers, of family, of history and community; yet she had a thoroughly international upbringing, in Libya and Turkey, where her father, the poet and translator Gwyn Williams, was professor of English. Later, after university at Bangor and Oxford, she taught for a couple of years in Bologna. She spoke several languages well, and lived a fully bilingual life through two of them, Welsh and English. In the rare moments of time she had for herself, on trains, between meetings, she jotted down bits of poems on the backs of envelopes in the language she loved best. There should have been many more like this. Lowri brought her vivid intelligence, shaped by many cultures and languages and places, back to nourish her Welsh heartland; translating her words opens them out once again to the world.

*Mae rhai o'r llinellau hyn yn dyddio o noswaith ddwy flynedd yn ôl,*
*ychydig ar ôl i ni fel teulu symud i Geredigion. Eleni, diolch i Restr*
*Testunau'r Eisteddfod ffeindion nhw ffurf filanèl, a beirniad caredig.*

## Dychwelyd

Ar gerrig caredig Ceredigion,
ar lonydd mynydd fy mhlentyndod i
mae meithrinfa fwynaf y ddaear hon.

Hafau yn nhai bach twt adfeilion,
heb nabod peryg, oedd fy chwarae i
ar gerrig caredig Ceredigion.

Codes fy mhac a ffoi ei threialon
ond er y crwydro, y diboblogi,
mae meithrinfa fwynaf y ddaear hon

yma o hyd yn gartre i'm meibion -
maen nhwythe'n cael braint eu mabinogi
ar gerrig caredig Ceredigion.

Derbynian nhw gyfocth a gofalon,
ond diolch mai yn ei chymdeithas hi
mae meithrinfa fwynaf y ddaear hon.

Heddiw yn dri ar draeth Aberaeron,
teimlwn dan draed yr haul a'i haelioni:
ar gerrig caredig Ceredigion
mae meithrinfa fwynaf y ddaear hon.

Some of the following lines date from an evening two years ago,
a short while after we had moved as a family to Ceredigion. This
year, thanks to the Eisteddfod's List of Titles, they found their
form as a villanelle, and a sympathetic judge.

# Returning

On Ceredigion's kindly cairns
and childhood's upland tracks
is mind and body's dearest home.

Summer in ruined rooms of fern;
my play knew nothing of the dark
on Ceredigion's kindly cairns.

The place had hurt; I learned
to leave. Generations packed
and left, but still my dearest home

is here, and living, for my loves:
my boys in flower, back
on Ceredigion's kindly cairns.

To them be goldenness. Cares
will come, but will not crack
the columns of this dearest home.

Today on Aberaeron beach, glare
and heat of sun on sand and back.
On Ceredigion's kindly cairns
is mind's, is body's, dearest home.

# Peruvian voices: *The poet's gun is a rose*
# Poems by Chabuca Granda and Javier
# Heraud
*Translated by Timothy Allen*

The three poems translated below are taken from the works of
two key figures in twentieth-century Peruvian life: Chabuca
Granda and Javier Heraud. Chabuca is the single most important
figure in the history of twentieth-century Peruvian music: her
most famous ballads ('La Flor de la Canela', 'Fina Estampa',
'José Antonio') are a lyrical celebration of Peru itself, with its
Inca heritage and its mixed population of indigenous peoples,
mestizos, criollos and Afro-Peruvians. Over her long career,
she first created and then transformed Peruvian popular music,
giving it a depth and a fluidity that has enabled her songs not
only to serve as a commentary on what it means to be Peruvian,
but even to become themselves an essential part of that national
identity. She remains the benchmark by which today's Peruvian
musicians are measured. In recent years, Susana Baca and Eva
Ayllón have both enjoyed success with covers of Chabuca's songs,
including versions of 'El fusil del poeta'.

By contrast, Javier Heraud is remembered as much for the
senseless tragedy of his violent death as for his precocious talent:
an award-winning poet by the age of eighteen, he was shot dead

by the Peruvian army at the age of twenty-one during a hare-brained attempt to instigate an armed uprising in the jungle close to the border with Bolivia. The manner of his death prefigured that of one of the figures he most admired: Che Guevara was killed by the Bolivian army in similar circumstances just four years later.

'El fusil del poeta es una rosa' is one of a series of songs Chabuca wrote in homage to that precocious but doomed young poet. The lyric lends itself both to translation and to adaptation as an on-the-page poem: its structure is remarkably free-form, given that it is a song, and its rhythms and cadences are shaped by the narrative of the event, rather than by any formal constraints. Although the song has a clarity that enables it to speak directly even to a reader/listener who knows nothing of its historical background, some knowledge of Javier Heraud's brief life and work helps shed more light on Chabuca's words, and not least the allusion she makes in the opening lines to one of Heraud's seemingly most prescient poems. 'Simplemente sucede,' she sings: 'It just so happens . . .' The force of this otherwise innocuous-sounding half-line is a reference whose force depends on its listeners' familiarity with Heraud's 'I never laugh about death'. It tells us a lot about Peruvians that Chabuca could expect them to know exactly what she was talking about.

The story of Javier Heraud can be quickly told. Born into a well-to-do liberal Limeñan family (his father was a prominent lawyer), at the age of sixteen Heraud became the youngest ever high school teacher in Peru, teaching courses in Spanish and English at two high schools to subsidise his own university studies. At the age of eighteen, he published *The River* (1960), the collection of poems that made him famous, and for which he shared (with César Calvo) an award for the most promising poets of their generation. In 1961, he published *The Journey*, which resulted in an International Youth Forum travel bursary that would change his life, taking him to Moscow, China, France, Spain and eventually Cuba, where he attended a course in cinema. These experiences shifted his politics further left: the young student who had demonstrated peacefully against Richard Nixon's 1961 visit now called himself a revolutionary. Alongside six similarly middle-class boys from Lima, in May 1963 he headed for Madre de Dios river, close to the Bolivian border, intending to encourage the local peasantry to join them in an armed uprising. All seven young men were shot dead by the Peruvian army, who believed they represented a much larger Soviet-backed force on the far side of the river; twenty-nine bullets were recovered from Heraud's body. He was just twenty-one years old.

Chabuca Granda's 'The poet's gun is a rose' neither glamorises Javier Heraud (she sees his disastrous foray into armed revolution as an extension of a children's game) nor belittles his achievement: 'He is still winning the war with his rose...' The song contains a sense that bullets may be more powerful than words on a battlefield, but that words will win out in the long run. She wrote and recorded it in 1968, a few months after Che Guevara had gone to his own death in an equally futile attempt to instigate an armed rebellion among the peasants of Bolivia. Che Guevara's image remains iconic among left-leaning youth all around the world; the name of Javier Heraud carries a similar resonance in twenty-first century Peru.

These three characters, in their various ways, seem so rooted in a distant and turbulent past that it can come as a jolt to realise that all three could very easily have lived to be part of our present. Chabuca Granda died of heart complications in 1983, after a career spanning half a century; had she lived, she would have been just ninety years old today. Che Guevara would have been eighty-two – a little older than President Raúl Castro, and a little younger than his brother Fidel. Javier Heraud – who died in a hail of bullets almost half a century ago – would be celebrating his seventieth birthday in 2012.

Presented here is a translation of Chabuca Granda's 'El fusil del poeta es una rosa', followed by versions of two of Javier Heraud's best-known poems. The first, 'El río', is the title poem from his prize-winning debut collection. In the second, 'Yo nunca me río de la muerte', Heraud envisages and accepts the idea of his own death. This is the poem to which Chabuca makes reference in her lament for the young poet.

### Further note from Tim Allen

Readers may find it interesting to see some quite rare footage of Chabuca herself singing another of her songs, *Fina Estampa (Handsome Face)*. She's 53 when this TV recording was made. http://www.youtube.com/watch?v=ggqPjptuxps (Coincidentally there's a Peruvian restaurant, named after this song, near Tower Bridge in south-east London.)

I've also found the following homage to Javier Heraud consisting of photographs of the poet with a soundtrack of two Chabuca songs dedicated to the poet (including *El fusil del poeta*): http://www.youtube.com/watch?v=ASQneSBKlCQ

Maybe the best interpreter of her songs is Eva Ayllón, who gave a concert of Chabuca's songs in Buenos Aires last year. Excerpts from this concert can be found here: http://www.youtube.com/watch?v=gMs9yJTKi5o&feature=related

## *Chabuca Granda*

## The poet's gun is a rose

While he played at war, the way children play,
making their guns out of any old thing –
who knows, from sticks of rice
or maybe even from a rose –
he grew up on love,

fired up with its furies.
And then one day
he signed up to die
in the place he wanted to die,
saying: 'I happen to be unafraid
of dying among trees and birds.'

That day, his gun was a rose
fired in the air. The rose was dangerous,
and the sun was the sun and the river was just
a river, but this time the game was war.
Death came out of that little brook, death rose
against his little gun (which on that day was only a rose)
but this game was war, and the sun was the sun
and the river a river, but this verse exploded
like a grenade. It opened like a rose, colouring
the waters of the river, its roots ran red
along the banks of the river, it settled like dew,
it felt like rain, or like the waters of a flooded
river, it opened up the broken veins
of the river, just as it then opened up
the breast of the poet.

He is still winning that war with his rose,
with the mouth of that river, its birds and its trees.
That day he played at war, the game that men play,
and he made his gun out of anything, or anything
that wasn't a gun. That day he was armed with a rose.
The poet's gun is just a rose.

## Javier Heraud

## The river

**1**
I am a river, going down over wide stones,
going down over hard rocks,
my path drawn by the wind.
The trees around me are shrouded with rain.
I am a river, descending with greater fury,
with greater violence,
whenever a bridge reflects me in its curves.

**2**
I am a river, a river.
A river: clear as crystal every morning.
Sometimes I am tender and kind.
I slide smoothly through fertile valleys.
I let the cattle and the gentle people
drink as much as they want.
Children run to me by day.
At night, trembling lovers stare into my eyes
and plunge themselves
into the stark darkness of my ghostly waters.

**3**
I am a river.
But sometimes I am wild and strong.
Sometimes I have no respect for life or death.
Cascading in furious waterfalls,
I beat those stones again and again,
I smash them into interminable pieces.
The animals run. They run.
They run when I flood their fields,

when I sow their slopes with tiny pebbles,
when I flood their homes and their meadows,
when I flood their doors and their hearts,
their bodies and their hearts.

### 4

And this is when I come down even faster:
when I can reach into their hearts
and grasp their very blood
and I can look at them from inside.
Then my fury turns peaceful
and I become a tree.
I seal myself up like a tree
and I turn silent as a stone
and I go quiet as a thornless rose.

### 5

I am a river.
I am the river of eternal happiness.
I feel the neighbourly breezes,
I feel the wind on my face, till my journey
– across mountains, rivers, lakes and prairies –
becomes endless.

### 6

I am the river that travels
along banks, past trees and dry stones,
I am the river that surges
through your ears, your doors, your open hearts.
I am the river that travels
by meadows, by flowers, by tended roses,
I am the river that travels
along streets, across earth, under drenched sky.
I am the river that travels
by mountains, rocks and burned salt.
I am the river that travels

through homes, tables, chairs.
I am the river that travels
inside men – tree, fruit, rose, stone,
table, heart, heart, door –
everything turned over.


7
I am the river that sings to people at midday.
I sing before their graves.
I turn my face towards those sacred places.


8
I am the river become night.
I go down by the broken depths,
by the forgotten unknown villages,
by the cities crammed to the very windows with people.
I am the river,
I flow through the prairies.
The trees on my banks are alive with doves.
The trees sing with the river,
the trees sing with my bird's heart,
the rivers sing with my arms.


9
The hour will come
when I will have to disperse
into the ocean,
to mix my clean waters with its murky waters.
I will have to silence my luminous song,
I will have to hush how I babble a hallo
to the dawn of each day,
I will wash my eyes with the sea.
That day will come,
and in those immense seas
I will no longer see my fertile fields,
I will never again see my green trees,

my neighbourly breeze,
my clear sky, my dark lake,
my sun, my clouds,
I will see nothing,
except that immense blue heaven
where everything is dissolved,
in that vast expanse of water,
where one more song or another poem
will mean nothing more
than a little river trickling down,
or a mighty river coming down to join me,
in my new luminous waters,
in my newly extinguished waters.

## *Javier Heraud*

# I never laugh about death.

I never laugh
about death.
It simply
happens that
I am not
afraid
to die
among
trees and birds.

I don't laugh about death.
But sometimes I get so thirsty
that I ask something from life.
Sometimes I get thirsty and I ask questions
every day, and what happens is
I get no answers
except a deep and dark
belly laugh. Like I say, I'm not in the habit
of laughing about death,
but even so, I know her white
face, her morbid clothes.

I don't laugh about death.
And yet I know her white house,
I know her white clothes,
I know her dampness and her silence.
It's true, of course, that death
hasn't visited me yet.
So you people will ask: *In that case*
*what exactly do you know?*

I don't know anything.
And that's true too.

And yet, I know that when she comes
I will be waiting for her.
I'll be waiting for her on foot
or maybe while having breakfast.
I will look at her blandly
(she won't scare me)
and since I have never laughed
at her costume, I will accompany her
all alone. All alone.

# Tal Nitzan
## 'Behind the eyelids'
### *Translated by Vivian Eden*

Tal Nitzan is an award-winning Israeli poet, editor and major translator of Hispanic literature. She has published four poetry collections and is the recipient of numerous awards, among them the Women Writers' Prize, the Culture Minister's Prize for Beginning Poets, the Debut Poetry Book Award, the Prime Minister's Writers' Prize.

Her work has been translated into several languages, and has appeared in anthologies in German, French and Lithuanian. An anthology of her poetry is forthcoming this year in Italy.

Nitzan edited the ground-breaking anthology *With an Iron Pen* (2005), a collection of Hebrew poems protesting against the Israeli occupation (published in English by SUNY Press, USA).

# Behind the eyelids

We've been trapped in the land of sleep.
Between my exile and yours,
on a street whose name rots in the rain
in a setting of child bicycle thieves
and baffling bedraggled women,
there one room is reserved for us,
twenty-four hours.
I immediately forgot the map you drew me –
if you close your eyes all is lost,
lost if you open them too.
And what is the lullaby
one voice will sing to us both
                    *A carousel of shadows*
*goes round and round.*
*Don't hold on, don't remember*
*get back to the ground*

There is no place for us in the waking hours.
Here, where summer's hand
reluctantly releases the throat and bats
hurl themselves high above the pavement
and are swallowed up in daylight,
only behind my eyelids can I see
the colour of your whisky, of your snow.
And you fall asleep while my body is terribly awake,
and leave as I sleep with my face towards the window.
What is the consolation
and what is the lullaby
that will awaken us both at once

*Night train*
*striving towards the light,*
*board it and leave*
*your body behind*

What I am not:
playing at has been or hasn't
wondering if you were real or imagined –
as though I could invent
the two different halves of your face,
as though my own two halves were true.
And like a guttering light bulb
your name is erased, recalled, erased,
sixty flickers per minute,
match to match, silence in silence
and what is the lullaby
that will cover us both in one single instant,
*with eyes open wide*
*in the hush that will dawn*
*dwindling away,*
*going, gone.*

# Sirkka Turkka
# Three poems from: *The Man Who Loved His Wife Too Much* (1979)
# *Translated by Emily Jeremiah*
# *(with Fleur Jeremiah)*

Sirkka Turkka (b. 1939) writes in a precise and lucid fashion. But her poems often relate utterly loopy things; the work is playful, bizarre. As Jukka Koskelainen notes in a recent piece for *Books from Finland*, it is also polyphonic; the poems contain numerous allusions to literature and culture, including popular culture; Turkka quotes pop songs, rock lyrics, the Bible, folklore, philosophical texts, and proverbs. The quotations form an organic part of the poems, but just a part; Turkka's own, strong voice is always discernible.

Koskelainen identifies cadence (in Finnish *poljento*) as key to the success of Turkka's poetry. Cadence, he notes, has to do with the possibilities of language. It involves the ability to create elliptical structures, recurring patterns, variations; and to keep all the ingredients together in a rhythmic whole. Tone is crucial here; in Turkka, irony and humour meet solemnity and formality, and the result is a rich and nuanced mélange of effects.

Koskelainen terms Turkka's aesthetic 'realism of the mind', for the poems are based largely on associations, following the flow

of thoughts freely. But the language is polished to the utmost.
While the poems feature the rhythm of spells, prayers, or folk
poetry, they are clearly distinct from such vernacular forms, being
sophisticated and honed. But these influences pervade Turkka's
poetry, which eludes rational understanding and yet hits home.

The poems feel utterly natural, although they are artful. Indeed,
they often have nature as a concern, and the animal/human
division is frequently blurred. But this is no romanticizing, twee
view of nature; rather it is robust and earthy. The poems draw
on cultural codes to depict nature, asserting the enmeshment of
nature and culture. The stars are like a tearful ballad; dogs tune
their violins. The poet asserts her right to live in the forest, green,
brown, and earth-coloured; and she does this through her art.

See: Jukka Koskelainen, 'Nature Girl: On the Poetry of Sirkka
Turkka', www.booksfromfinland.fi (2010).

## Once more the stars are like a tearful ballad . . .

Once more the stars are like a tearful ballad, and always in
    the evenings
the dogs tune their cracked violins.
I don't allow grief to come,
I don't let it near.
A thousand metres of snow on the heart.
I mutter a lot to myself, I sing aloud
in the street.
Sometimes I see myself in passing, a hat on my head, real
    fodder
for the wind, and some thought askew.
I speak of death when I mean life. I roam with mixed-up

papers, I own no theory, only a cursing dog.
When I ask for spirits, I'm given ice-cream,
I suppose I'm Spanish then, hairline
so low like this, really:
I can't be from round here.
I sweat and try to speak, or then at times
I shiver.
Nearly more than death, I grieve my birth.
And all I ask for is
a thousand metres of snow on the heart.


## At six o' clock in the evening . . .


At six o'clock in the evening, the conductor walks,
holding a bottle of spirits. Far away from here,
in Czechoslovakia, he's conducting an orchestra.
They get the idea there, he and his dear head:
a flimsy barn traversed by flying
philosophies and bicycles, French and Dutch ones
with ten gears, spare parts and technicians.
It's six o'clock in the evening and already
I'm an orphan, thanks to the
hefty cow, between whose horns the poem withers.
Everyone turns their back on me,
waiter, I kiss your glass; mongrel and snotty
door-mat.
And still I'm a candidate,
a scar on my arm, woven by fire
into the flesh. And although perhaps I loved, although I
    wasn't able to,
I am known for this: for the scar woven by fire
into the flesh.

# Today I stumbled over a branch . . .

Today I stumbled over a branch and the path, the forest's own
    river,
hit me in the heart with its moss-fist.
I gasped there for a moment.
An animal always rejoices, encountering food,
it sings about it, even after eating.
They say I have eyes like a bird of prey, a tiger:
a yellow ring circles the iris.
I'm just as blue-eyed as the cornflower
edging the underside of the sky.
I am green and brown in the snow, always earth-coloured.
A large hand has often tried
to wipe me away
like a now-useless tear, with the corner of a handkerchief.
It has tried in earnest.
But again and again I've wrested back
the right to live
so green, so brown,
in the forest, after its fashion, on the earth, earth-coloured.
I am mild to the mild, you can't deceive me.
I look the animal in the eye and the millennia speak silently.
I'm tired, old as a thousand years,
but never so ready for battle as now.
A feather in the heart or a predator's tooth.
Ready to be stroked or struck.
Without faltering, quickly.
Alone and now.

# Surjit Patar
# 'The Magician of Words'
## *Translated by Amarjit Chandan*

**Translator's Note:**

Surjit Patar and I are contemporaries. Patar excels in the *ghazal* genre and sings on the stage. Singing poetry in public without musical instruments is called *tarranum* (from the Arabic for 'melody') which is unique to Punjabi and Urdu poetry. The audience, unlike North Europeans, responds to the poet in a lively way. However this experiential poem is written in free verse. The powerful impact of the poem read by Patar with Spanish translation in the Medellin World Poetry Festival can be seen on You Tube: http://www.youtube.com/watch?v=pSg4HjoIn K0&feature=related

Surjit Patar has published four books of poems and has translated three tragedies of Lorca and poems by Brecht and Neruda into Punjabi. He has also adapted plays by Euripides, Racine and Giraudoux. In 1995, he was given the Sahitya Akademi (Indian Academy of Letters) Award, and the Saraswati Award by the KK Birla Foundation India this year.

# The Magician of Words

I was sitting in Obrero Park in the town of Medellin
    in Colombia.
I was there to attend a poetry festival.

A child came to me riding his bike.
Looking at my turban and beard he asked me:
Are you a magician?

I was about to say: No I am not.
But I didn't feel like saying so.

I said: Yes.
I can pluck stars from the heavens
    to make necklaces for girls.
I can turn trees into musical instruments
    and the leaves into tunes.
I can make the air the fingertips of the guitar player.
I can transform the wounds into flowers.

The child was enthralled and asked me: Really?
If so, can you turn my bike into a horse?

Thinking for a moment I said:
I do not make magic for children.
I do it for adults.

Then can you turn my mama and papa's house into a palace?

I am not a magician of things.
I play magic with words.

*Ya lo sé, usted es poeta.*
Now I know, you are a poet.
Saying this waving at me and smiling
    he cycled off out of the park
and entered into my poem.

# Reesom Haile
# Three poems
## *Translated by Charles Cantalupo*

---

Reesom Haile was Eritrea's first internationally known poet. He wrote in Tigrinya, one of Eritrea's nine major languages. In exile during Eritrea's war for independence from Ethiopia, he served for over two decades as a Development Communications consultant, working with UN Agencies, governments and NGOs around the world before returning to Eritrea in 1994. His first collection of Tigrinya poetry, *Waza ms Qum Neger nTensae Hager* (1997), won the Raimok prize, Eritrea's highest award for literature. He published two other books of poetry, translated by Charles Cantalupo and published by Red Sea Press – *We Have Our Voice* (2000) and *We Invented the Wheel* (2002) before he died in 2003.

## emrom tHSer

swuatna
gdam Hadirom
san zQebrom

meraHtna
gdam Hadirom
seKirom

nseKirom
zbluna neKbrrom
Emrom tHSer Emrom

## The Dead of the Night

Out all night,
Our unburied martyrs
Decay.

Out all night,
Our country's leaders
Get drunk.

'Honour our leaders,'
You say?
Let them pass away.


## sAt koynom sAt!

ab Hanti amet
Hanti meSHaf
ab mongom
ente anbibom
men kemom!

feliTeyom
bakWeraryom

Hgi eblom Hgi
gzieu aykonen ybluni

ftHi eblom ftHi
gzieu aykonen ybluni

srAt eblom srAt eblom
gzieu aykonen ybluni

sAt koynom sAt!
men kon yKewn zmelom?

## Are They Watches?

They only read
What they have written.
Ask the time.
They only tell themselves.

Say, 'What about the law?'
And they answer,
'Now is not the time for that.'

Say you want justice,
And you hear,
'It's not yet the right time.'

Ask for order,
And they answer,
'The time for order has not
come.'

Are they watches,
Waiting to be wound?

## elohie ! elohie !

elohie ! elohie ! lmnte
hadegkeni !
mebeliKa krstos loms
beSiHuni!

kWulaso kab engieray
mAgo kab mayey
TAmo endo sQayey

nsKas teferidka frdi bQienanu
teasirom enewulka
y,eseru alewulka deqi Adey
jeganu

qWeSeraKe qWeSera nfrdi
bQienanu
abey alewu Kbleka abeyo
endyom seb zdagWnu

elohie ! elohie ! lmnte
hadegkeni !
mebeliKa krstos loms
beSiHuni !

## Jesus' Last Words

'My God, my God,
Why hast thou forsaken me?"
You said it, Jesus.
Now I see what you mean.

How's this for bread?
Taste this cup.
Talk about pain?

Your court was crooked,
But at least you got a trial.
My heroes rot in jail,
Or tomorrow they're locked
up –

Nobody knows where,
And the court doesn't care.
It sets no trial date.

'My God, my God,
Why hast thou forsaken me?'
You said it, Jesus.
Now I see what you mean.

# Naomi Jaffa
# Aldeburgh 2010: the ultimate polyphonic poetry experience

*Modern Poetry in Translation*'s theme of 'Polyphony' lends itself perfectly to the concept of a poetry festival and is certainly at the heart of the programming principles at Aldeburgh each year. Poetry is customarily thought of as a solitary pursuit, the voice of the poet being equivalent to that of musical soloist rather than ensemble player. But in the context of the Aldeburgh weekend, poetry becomes a collective pleasure – as an attender once wrote: 'the festival brings poetry out of the book, the library, the private place, and celebrates it.'

'Polyphony' of course usually refers to music and is defined as 'two or more independent melodic parts sounding together'. But at Aldeburgh – where we're not on the experimental edge of presenting poets reading simultaneously – the polyphonic effect is linear and progressive.

It starts with the major readings which always feature three poets. Since Aldeburgh began in 1989, these core 'three-handers' have formed the pillars on which the rest of the programme is built. The principles are simple and effective: we research and invite an unusual and never-repeated mix of writers – established and less well-known UK names, new and overlooked talent, international voices and always poets in translation with their translators – to generate surprising combinations which guarantee variety and discoveries. Themes emerge, connections are made and individual voices grow both distinctive and intertwined as the programme gathers its own momentum.

And Aldeburgh is much more than straight readings. The programme – in many ways resembling a musical score – allows poets to come in at different points and demonstrate tonal range. As individuals: for 15-minute close readings of touchstone poems; introductions to presiding spirits (e.g. Marie Howe on Stanley Kunitz); and half-hour craft talks considering different aspects of technique (e.g. John Irons on issues of translation). In pairs for exchanges: Selima Hill and Bill Manhire on whether happiness writes white; Lars Gustafsson and Bernard Kops on the subversive poet. And in panels (including Inua Ellams, Elaine Feinstein and Andrew Motion) to discuss the essentials of 'The Poet's Toolkit' on Saturday morning, and on Sunday the attractions of other kinds of writing.

As well as poets from Sweden (Lars Gustafsson) and The Netherlands (Toon Tellegen), there'll be many different kinds of English on offer, including East End Jewish (Bernard Kops), Dundee Scottish (Don Paterson), Dublin Irish (Harry Clifton). And from much further, America's Marie Howe and Dorianne Laux and New Zealand's Bill Manhire.

For the ultimate oral/aural polyphonic poetry experience, it's got to be Aldeburgh throughout the first weekend each November.

22<sup>nd</sup> Aldeburgh Poetry Festival, 5–7 November 2010
full details available from www.thepoetrytrust.org
for a printed programme or further information:
info@thepoetrytrust.org or 01986 835950

# Lars Gustafsson
# Two poems
*Translated by John Irons*

Born in 1936, Lars Gustafsson is one of the most prolific Swedish writers since August Strindberg. Since the late 1950s he has produced a voluminous flow of poetry, novels, short stories, critical essays and editorials. He taught Philosophy and Creative Writing at the University of Texas from 1982 until his retirement in 2006 and he is one of the few Swedish writers to have gained international recognition – with major literary awards including a Guggenheim Fellowship for poetry in 1994 and a Nobel nomination. Translated into fifteen languages, Gustafsson appears at Aldeburgh with his English translator John Irons who has been professionally translating poetry – mainly from Dutch and the Scandinavian languages – for 20 years.

Irons confesses to being 'a compulsive translator – if I like poems in a collection, I often translate the whole collection, to try and work my way into the feel of things. Each poet is a new dialect for me – I have to be able to hear the pulse of the poetry inside me before I can translate. So the more "dialect" I have available for translation, the greater the chance of getting the pulse right.' Irons was first attracted by Gustafsson's 'capacity to create pictures in my mind. He can paint the surface of things vividly, but also suggest the depths that lie under the surface.' Writing about the experience of translating Gustafsson's most recent collection *A Time in Xanadu* (Copper Canyon Press 2008), Irons comments on 'the wide range of forms and lengths – even some prose poems. But there IS a pulse to be found. It's a bit like the Goldberg Variations. No matter the different tempi, there is a pulse running through all the poems.'

# On the richness of the inhabited worlds

In some worlds one has confirmed
Riemann's prime number conjecture

In some worlds one extracts
lengthy confessions from ancient fungi

In a certain world the profound darkness
is transilluminated by wonderful talking stones

In quite a few worlds summer lasts
a century, and those unfortunate enough

to be born during the winter century
spend their lives sleeping

suspended in fur-lined
light-grey cocoons

In some worlds even this poem has
already been written by various poets

# The lamp

Before the lamp was lit
we sat completely still

A crow's rasping voice
and a sudden scent of clover

with a sweetish warmth
through this rising dark.

Water, completely still.
The earth, it too tranquil.

The bird flew
as close as it could

over its own shadow

And the bumblebee, faithful
friend of many summers,

crashed against the window pane
as if it were the wall of the world

And the dive dapper
flew from lake to lake

It could be late
or early
in various lives in various lives

it could be in a butterfly's shadow
In the shadow of any life.

# Toon Tellegen
# Two poems
*Translated by Judith Wilkinson*

Toon Tellegen was born in Den Briel, The Netherlands in 1941
and studied medicine at Utrecht and Rotterdam Universities.
After practical training for the tropics, he moved to Kenya where
for over three years he worked in a hospital in Maasai country
before returning to live in Amsterdam where he combines his
professional lives as both practising GP and writer. A novelist,
playwright and well-known children's writer, Tellegen considers
himself first and foremost a poet and has published more than
twenty poetry collections. *About love and about nothing else* – his
first selected poems translated into English – was published by
Shoestring Press in 2008.

In her introduction, translator Judith Wilkinson describes
Tellegen's poetry as 'one of movement, of surprising leaps, of
living speech full of impatient interruptions and impetuous
questions... it defies comparison with that of any other Dutch
poet and should perhaps be seen in a broader European context.'
Offering further amplification: 'Tellegen's work remains difficult
to pin down. One might recognise some of the candour and
immediacy of Catullus, something of Cavafy's colloquial tone
and ironic perspective, something of de Saint-Exupéry's sense
of wonder and childlike simplicity.' On her translation process,
Wilkinson's intention is to keep the language 'as unencumbered
as that of the original texts, remaining close to spoken language
in its most concrete form. In terms of the whole rhythm and
structure of the poems, I have closely followed the originals and
have aimed at keeping the English as dynamic and dramatic as
the Dutch.'

# A man and an angel fought in silence, fiercely . . .

A man and an angel fought in silence, fiercely,
it isn't fair, said the man,
no, it isn't fair, said the angel
with a peculiar celestial accent

the sun was shining, the horizon trembled,
small planes with day-glo wings wrote in the sky,
in capitals:

     IT ISN'T FAIR

and schoolmistresses with chapped lips
dictated to children with tearful faces:

it isn't fair,
it wasn't fair,
it will never be fair

once, biting his terrible nails,
God saw that it was good,
but not fair

the man looked up
and the angel struck him down.

# A man collected questions, uncertainties . . .

A man collected questions, uncertainties,
vague inklings, dubious assumptions,
wrong-headed conclusions, debatable motives,
misplaced convictions, mood swings,
painful states of mind, feverish fluctuations in character
and unremitting, conflicting thoughts about death

collected himself into the ground

and an angel touched him very gently, very carefully
and with the greatest possible tenderness
and autumn came
and the wind lifted the man up and blew him away

children, a few small children, caught a last glimpse of him
    dancing
on the rays
of the setting sun.

The Launch of 'Transplants' *Modern Poetry in Translation* Series 3, Number 13

12 May 2010

at the LRB Bookshop

*Photos by Amarjit Chandan*

Allen Prowle and
Carmela Biscaglia

Carol Rumens

Shazea Quraishi

Maureen Duffy

# Reviews

*Fernando Pessoa*
*The Collected Poems of Álvaro de Campos Vol.2: 1928-1935*
Translated by Chris Daniels
Shearsman Books
198 pp, paperback, £12.95
ISBN 978-1-905700-25-7

Unlike a pseudonym, or an anonym, the heteronym is a wholly fabricated persona: the author is not writing as himself under another or a concealed name, he is writing *as* another character altogether. An exact contemporary of T.S. Eliot, Fernando Pessoa was born in Lisbon in 1888; he died young, at forty-seven, of cirrhosis of the liver. He published in his own name and also created dozens of literary alter egos in his short lifetime. Some wrote prose, others, such as Alexander Search, wrote poems in English (Pessoa emigrated to South Africa as a child, returning to Portugal in his teens, and was therefore fluent). All his personas had individual biographies, poetics, preoccupations and styles: Álvaro de Campos, Alberto Caeiro and Ricardo Reis being the most prolific and inter-referential.

Anyone with an urge to learn more about the effusive, extravagantly confessional, 'sensationist' verse of Campos would do well to read the letters he wrote to his contemporary and 'master' Caeiro. In turn, those with an interest in Caeiro's bucolic

opus as the 'absolute essence of paganism' should refer to the
rigorous introductory essays of the neo-classical formalist Reis.
To know something of Fernando Pessoa, it is advisable to read
some of all three... And thus a corner of the irresistibly complex
heteronymical project that has defined Pessoa as the father of
Portuguese modernism unfolds.

Campos – a one time naval engineer who trained in Glasgow
and lived in England before returning to Lisbon – made his debut
in Pessoa's controversial literary journal *Orpheu* in 1914. Pessoa
continued to attribute poems to Campos until his (Pessoa's) death
in 1935.

This chronologically organised volume comprises the latter
part of his output; together with Volume I it will be 'the first-
ever collected edition of Campos' work in English' and forms
part of Shearsman's Pessoa series, which includes *The Collected
Poems of Alberto Caeiro*, also translated by Chris Daniels. As such,
the poems in this individual volume are, like their author, just
one part of a polyphonous and multi-faceted whole.

Some 27,543 documents and 70+ heteronyms are thought to
make up the body of Pessoa's work, which he kept in a large
wooden trunk. Many of the Campos poems are dated yet
untitled; one, it is noted, is written on the back of an envelope,
and viewed here they add to the pervasive feel of the collection
as an intimate, uncensored journal that has just been unearthed
from the bottom of that large trunk. No thought or detail that
crosses Campos' mercurial, and regularly tormented, mind is left
unuttered.

In the opening long poem 'Tobacco Shop' the first four lines
announce both the collection itself and allude – as do many of the
poems herein – to the heteronymical project.

I'm nothing.
I'll never be anything.
I can't wish I were anything.
Even so, I have all the dreams of the world in me.

The relationship between dreams and reality, madness and sanity is an enduring fascination for Campos (early poems cast him as an alternately indolent and frustrated opium addict) and later, as a poet endeavouring to make sense of life's existential dualities, as in poems such as 'Typing' (1933):

We all have two lives:
The true one we dream in childhood
And continue to dream as adults in a misty substrate;
The false one we live among others,
The practical life, the useful life –
It ends up sticking us in a coffin.

Campos referred to himself as a 'sensationist' poet, one whose commitment to an often melancholic poetry of the senses overshadowed all other enquiry. Almost invariably he wrote in *vers libre*, the lines long and meandering and often anaphoric; Walt Whitman's *Leaves of Grass* was said to be one of Campos' (and Pessoa's) early and defining influences. Here, the effect is an intense musicality and at times an almost breathless stream of consciousness. In his brief Translator's Notes (a longer introduction will, presumably, appear in Volume I, which is forthcoming) Chris Daniels says he left the punctuation intact so Anglophone readers could enjoy Campos 'as is'. This seems an astute decision, as it is perhaps by retaining the original syntax that Daniels achieves a naturalness and ease that suits both Campos' voice and philosophy.

Freedom is what Campos seeks: 'No! All I want is freedom!/ Love, glory, money – they're prisons', he exclaims in an untitled poem from 1930; and freedom is also what the heteronym bestows on Pessoa himself. Daniels notes that Campos is thought to have been the person Pessoa would have most liked to have been. Ironically, of course Pessoa *was* Campos, but it is arguably the separation of the poet from the heteronym that empowers the work. It is perhaps because Campos is only *one* aspect of multiple poetic personalities that he feels able to express his

thoughts and feelings so emphatically. The pretence allows him
to be himself.

The poems also exhibit an indulgence that is at once a witty
self-parody and a means of exposition that Pessoa uses to create
the Campos character, as he does here in 'Oxfordshire':

I'm universally uncomfortable, metaphysically uncomfortable,
But the hell of it is I've got a headache.
That's more serious than the meaning of the Universe.

But if we are to laugh at Campos with Pessoa, the joke is
a good humoured and playful one. Campos is nothing if not
sincere and at the heart of Pessoa's endeavour was a deeply serious
poetic that sought to explore and create art/poetry as an act of
spiritual expression. However, the road to Ithaca – or in this case
Sintra – was rocky and the question of god(s)/faith versus logic a
maddeningly insoluble one that he explores in conversation with
his large and interconnected dramatis personae. 'My conscious
soul is such an ache in my real stomach!' Campos writes in
'Trolley Stop' – but, as he concludes in 'Quasi', 'Like a god, I
never straightened anything out, not my life, not the truth.'

*Karen McCarthy*


**Paschalis Nikolaou and Maria-Venetia Kyritsi**
**With a foreword by Mona Baker**
*Translating Selves: Experience and Identity between*
*Languages and Literatures*
Continuum
202 pp, hardback, ISBN 978-0-8264-9926-4

As the full title of this collection of essays suggests, 'translating
selves' are encountered in contexts in which languages, literatures
and cultures meet. These are 'ways of thinking, practices and
understandings, creativity and experiences that (re)define the

translating consciousness and (literary) translation' (p. 2). In an attempt to bring these selves to the foreground, it is crucial to challenge the boundaries of translation studies and invite studies from various fields such as comparative literature, cognitive science, creativity studies, discourse analysis, philosophy, and life-writing. The result here is a dynamic collection of essays born in the interfaces between such disciplines and will therefore largely appeal to researchers working in them as well as to the general reader keen to engage with issues relating to translation and intercultural communication.

The realisation that there has been 'relative neglect of the drives of the (literary) translator, the inner workings of his or her consciousness' (p. 3) in research narratives that focus on 'the bigger picture of literary systems, cultural encounters and theories of language' is intimated by the different chapters of this book. Thus the activity of translating, though historically conditioned to suppress the translator's subjectivity, is seen here as a process by which other selves – 'minds and sensibilities' (p. 9) – are internalised; it is 'an act coinciding with subtle disclosures of experience; a metaphor for, *a wording for*, the life lived between languages'.

*Translating Selves* is divided into three parts. First: ways of seeing, self, translation and the literary; secondly: language and translating between cultures and identities; and finally a series of four case studies focusing on the experience of translating a variety of texts that explore the idea of self in different cultural settings – from that of minority languages, such as Scottish Gaelic, to that of the migrant identity of the bicultural self, passing through the liminal space inhabited by the bilingual/bicultural writer/ translator to the space, or 'no-space' of the ineffable idea of self from Patañjali's *Yogas tra*. In the Foreword by Mona Baker, one of the keynote speakers at the Post Graduate Symposium held at the University of East Anglia in early February 2006 from which this book originates, the idea of a major reassessment of the role of the translating self, as well as that of the researching self, is highlighted, inviting the exploration of how these subjectivities shape the course and outcome of the work undertaken. The importance of such a procedure cannot be overestimated, since it is increasingly common to find that practitioners of (literary) translation also conduct research in the field of translation.

Various views of translation and translation theories surface as the different contributors explore their subject matter. Particularly mind-opening and provocative is Clive Scott's essay and rendering of Apollinaire's 'Les Fenêtres'. The self of the translator is seen as in suspension, as it awaits to be defined by the translational act. Yet this 'selving' of the translator is resisted by three forces; the 'uncontrollable selves of language', the 'selves of other speakers' resulting from the particular nature of this 'conversation-poem' which affirms their presence – the 'third-personness common to the intertextuality of all texts' (p.37) – as well as the reader's subjectivity. From the interplay of these forces comes a fascinating study of the process of rendering Apollinaire's poem in a way that shows 'the poet/translator re-launch[ing] language in all its multiplicity, and that multiplicity will not fulfil itself, realize itself, unless the poet/translator, to a degree, lets go, lets semantics recede to yield the field to the complexity of language's play' (p. 41). Thus, the last couple of lines in Apollinaire's 'Les Fenêtres':

La fenêtre s'ouvre comme une orange
Le beau fruit de la lumière

become, in Clive Scott's re-writing

The *window opens like an* ooorange
*The windows of my poetry are wide open to the boulevards and in its shop windows*
The plump *fruit* of **LIGHT**

Worth noting here is that a further book has resulted from this translational approach – *One Poem in Search of a Translator: Rewriting 'Les Fenêtres' by Apollinaire* (Edited by E.Loffredo and M. Perteghella). Another challenging essay is Maria Filippakopoulou's

'Translation drafts and the Translating Self' as she calls into question the insistence, in the field of translation studies, on focusing on the finished product, rather than on the translation process. Thus, the claim that translation drafts are a worthy object for research is validated as she proceeds to analyse the advantages and disadvantages of such methodology and arrives at the conclusion that 'translational writing is made up of two moments: the linguistic and the psychological, or the rhetoric and the ethical' (p. 34). Paschalis Nikolaou's explorations into the liaisons of literary translation and life-writing are also worth highlighting – one of the main tenets of this book is succinctly expressed thus: 'if writing partly creates the sense of self, the act of translation offers further ways of sustaining, enriching and multiplying it' (p. 55).

It is impossible to do justice to all the chapters in this volume in a single review. Each article makes a valuable contribution to our understanding of the idea of the multiple selves of translators and how they operate in the interface of languages and cultures. I'd like to close this review by referring to Paul Ricoeur's paradigmatic reflections on translation and his idea of 'linguistic hospitality' from an essay whose inclusion in this volume might invite some questioning from some readers as it is largely to do with Ricoeur's philosophical *oeuvre*: 'linguistic hospitality, where the pleasure of dwelling in the other's language is balanced by the pleasure of receiving the foreign word at home, in one's welcoming house' (p. 82, quoted from Ricoeur [2006] *On Translation*). Thus, the task of the translator becomes an ethical question – how to practise this linguistic hospitality. Worth remembering here is that Ricoeur's 'other' includes all possible forms of alterity the self meets: its body, its conscience (p. 83). Viewed thus, this volume has taken a step forward in bringing these forms of alterity together in the reflection on and around the writing of translations.

*Cecilia Rossi*

David Constantine
Notes on three books

Ingeborg Bachmann
*Kriegstagebuch. Mit Briefen von Jack Hamesh an Ingeborg Bachmann*
Hrsg. und mit einem Nachwort von Hans Höller
Suhrkamp Verlag Berlin 2010
108 pp. hardback ISBN 978-3-518-42145-1

The most poignant paragraphs of Ingeborg Bachmann's *War Diary* describe her brief friendship with the young Jewish Field Security Officer Jack Hamesh who had escaped from Austria in 1938 and returned with the British occupying forces in 1945. A year later, in love with her, he emigrated to Palestine. This neat volume brings together Bachmann's diary and the few letters and notes Hamesh wrote to her in 1946-7. Hans Höller's Afterword locates and connects this episode in Bachmann's life and work.

Thanks to the generosity of Heinz Bachmann and his sister Isolde Moser the *Kriegstagebuch* was first published entire in *MPT* 3/3 (2005) in an English translation, with a commentary, by Mike Lyons; and two of the fullest of Hamesh's letters (numbers 6 and 11 in this volume) had their first publication, translated, in *MPT* 3/9 (2008). Now a little more of the story is known and the figurative sense of Jack Hamesh and Ingeborg Bachmann and the poignancy of their encounter in that time, in those circumstances, are enhanced.

Daniel Huws
*Memories of Ted Hughes 1952-1963*
Richard Hollis Five Leaves Publications 2010
54 pp. paperback ISBN 978 1 905512 75 1

Daniel Huws appeared in the the third issue of *MPT* (spring 1967) with two dozen translations of poems by Ingeborg Bachmann and again in *MPT* 7 (June 1970) with another four. So, with Richard

Hollis, *MPT's* designer and the publisher of this memoir, and with Ted Hughes, its subject, he was in at our beginning. He first met Hughes at Cambridge, in the autumn of 1952, after a reading by Dylan Thomas, and was often in his company after that, in the Anchor, for example, the pub by Queen's Bridge. Then in London, Cambridge, and Wales he and his wife Helga knew Hughes and Sylvia Plath together, until Plath's death. This deeply sympathetic account is remarkable (in the context of the Hughes-Plath industry, quite extraordinary) for its tact, reticence, self-effacing modesty, intelligence and insight. There are many affecting moments: 'My last sight of her [Plath] was sitting bolt upright and staring ahead as the taxi vanished down the Kings Road. Soon afterwards she wrote a couple of very warm letters. Then I too, as everyone would do, inevitable though it may have been, managed to let her down.' He noted in Hughes a gift for bringing out the gifts in others. Hughes gave him and Luke Myers each a notebook, saying: 'Fill this with poems'. He comments: 'mine took ten or more years to fill.' Hughes was, he says, 'a forceful maker of suggestions, determined that people should turn their energy into creative channels.' One instance? 'He sensed Daniel Weissbort's true bent and with him began the lastingly influential *Modern Poetry in Translation.*'

There is much matter in this small book, which is available from Five Leaves Publications PO Box 8786, Nottingham NG1 9AW info@fiveleaves.co.uk

*Saudade. An Anthology of Fado Poetry*
Edited by Mimi Khalvati
Selected by Vasco Graça Moura
Calouste Gulbenkian Foundation 2010-08-25
190 pp. £8.50 ISBN 978 1 903080 13 9

This is a bi-lingual volume, original poems and their translations on facing pages, thirty-three Portuguese poets distributed among eighteen translators, many of them past and

present contibutors to *MPT*. Fado is a genre of urban popular
song and the translators were given not just texts but also a
CD of *fadistas* singing what they, the translators, would have to
put into words on a page. All translators of poetry must ask
themselves, 'Is this fit to be read? Read aloud?' Here also came
the question, 'Is this, in your words, fit to be sung?' Andrew
Barnett, UK Director of the Gulbenkian Foundation, is right to
say in his Preface: '*Saudade* has become a work about translation
itself.' There is a tradition of competitive improvisation in Fado,
called *desgarrada*. One *fadista* sings against another, taking up
and answering back. Rather as many of the translators do here,
and not just here. *Desgarrada* is no bad image for the whole
sport and struggle of poetic translation. *Saudade* means 'longing'.
Mimi Khalvati had the word more closely defined for her by
Isabel Lucena at the Foundation. Mimi writes: 'I had my first real
inkling of its sensation when Isabel pointed out that "longing"
reaches outwards, looks beyond horizons, whereas *saudade* – and
here she clasped her hands close to her heart – is holding the
object of your longing close to you, cherishing it, drawing it ever
deeper inwards.' *Saudade* is a wonderful anthology, so various in
its subjects, tones and voices. Buy it, read it, and if possible hear
the singers sing.

(Go to http://www.youtube.com/ , enter the word 'Fado' and there
are performances by a number of singers. Good sites to buy Fado
are Amazon for CDs www.amazon.com and iTunes for the digital
option http://www.apple.com/itunes/ At iTunes you can listen to
a sample of the track. Among CDs 'The Rough Guide to Fado' is
particularly recommended.)

*David Constantine*

# Further Reviews

**Ishikawa Takuboku**
*On Knowing Oneself Too Well, Selected Poems,* translated by Tamae
  K. Prindle
Syllabic Press
142 pp, paperback, ISBN 978-0-615-34562-8, $16.95

**Tsvetanka Elenkova**
*The Seventh Gesture,* translated by Jonathan Dunne
Shearsman Books
89pp, paperback, ISBN 978-1-84861-084-2, £8.95

**Lars Amund Vaage**
*Outside the Institution, Selected Poems,*
translated by Hanne Bramness and Frances Presley
Shearsman Books
104pp, paperback, ISBN 978-1-84861-075-0, £9.95 / $17

**András Mezei**
*Christmas in Auschwitz,* translated by Thomas Ország-Land
Smokestack Books
74pp, paperback, ISBN 978-0-9560341-9-9, £7.95

In this issue's round-up, four distinct and celebrated poets, yet
relatively unknown outside their homelands of Japan, Bulgaria,
Norway, and Hungary, are brought side by side in a polyphony of
spoken and unspoken truths on the texture of existence.

Ishikawa Takuboku's selected poems *Knowing Oneself Too
Well* poignantly illuminates the private self; its revelations, its
discomforts, its ordinary pleasures are succinctly observed,
confronted and brought home to rest in a collection of tanka
sequences and free-verse poems. Takuboku was born in 1885 in
Hinoto Village in Northern Japan, and though widely regarded

as one of Japan's most important modern poets, there is a notable absence of grandiosity in the work. Unfortunately, Takuboku lived only twenty-six years and it is unavoidable that these poems read as a testimony to a life cut short by tuberculosis.

Takuboku's acute sensibility moves through the poems whilst walking through the ordinariness of life. Each short tanka is individually and collectively irresistible and intimate. Each word, each phrase, breathes with a sense of grace and polite candour. Step by step the poems unfold like private daydreams, accumulating like a postcard sequence, depicting a state of knowing, an amused self gently awakening. Takuboku's impassioned, unquestioning soul leaves footprints on invisible paper:

> The blue ink
> Split on the frosted flagstone
> Below a bank's window . . .

> In the morning air of October,
> For the first time,
> A baby breathed.

> The pacing to and fro
> In the long wet hallway
> Of a gynecologist's office in October . . .

> There was a thought
> Tender like the touch of an infant
> When I walked alone in the park.
>                           ('When I take my gloves off')

A state of translucency has been quietly achieved in these sensitive translations by Tamae K. Prindle, her careful rendering in English of these works has not disturbed Takuboku's original interests and intentions: quietly bleeding through rice paper Takuboku's soothing voice confirms that there is a knowing self that delicately endures whilst bearing witness to the fullness and emptiness of life, until it ceases to be.

Holding hands with Death, each thumb and finger tightly locked, is the overriding action that resonates most strongly in Tsvetanka Elenkova's *The Seventh Gesture*. Despite this collection appearing in its original tongue in 2005, Elenkova's concerns still appear lively. Elenkova was born in Sofia in 1968 on the threshold of Bulgarian Orthodox tradition and contemporary culture, painful transitions and transformations come as second nature.

In his enigmatic Translator's Foreword, Jonathan Dunne sets the tone for meeting these poems head on: 'This book taught me to find life in death, a dead tree bathed in light. This book taught me to follow the diffraction of light in a bruise . . .' Dunne's translations occupy a sense of duality; he operates on the cusp of prose and poetry, on the hinges of an English welcome and Bulgarian hospitality. The poem's dual nature dances delightedly through each imagistic discovery as if by magic as in the opening poem: 'Poetry's tail':

You wave the wand and know exactly where the wave will end. As the artist strokes a brush across the canvas, as the conductor signals *allegro vivace,* as the godmother turns the pumpkin into a carriage. You stop suddenly but smoothly, gradually tapering off.

The closing sentence of the poem offers a wry glimpse of Bulgarian humour: 'But what's most important – the curve at the end. The Bulgarians incorporated it into the buckles of their belts . . .'

Reading *The Seventh Gesture* is a cinematic experience. From a close shot to a long shot, a wider action takes place in each of these breathless prose poems, extending beyond the *now* into the residues of time, the throb of each moment is palpable as well as its demise:

They find dead victims like this, with legs outstretched and
arms to the side. Children sleep like this in their sweetest
dreams. Like this, hung on a hook against you, I writhe at
your every touch.

('Day Four – Leonardo's Cross')

The reader is asked to temporarily suspend any form of
knowingness and surrender disbelief, giving over to Elenkova's
imagistic sensibility, which twists and unfolds with full confidence
in its linguistic responsibilities and pulsating actions.

Lars Amund Vaage's much-awaited *Selected Poems* is the first
translated collection to appear in English; it contains selections
from Vaage's most recent book *Outside the Institution* and poems
from his first collection *The Other Room* (2001). Vaage was born
in 1952 in Sunde on the west coast of Norway and is one of
the country's highly regarded, award-winning novelists. Vaage's
oeuvre stretches beyond prose to playwriting, a jazz requiem
and several translations of works by Lorine Niedecker and Joy
Harjo.

Arguably, the poems that continue to linger in the mind are
from Vaage's first collection. The poems in *The Other Room* are
lined with crystal clear imagery that glides effortlessly on ice
aided by the sharpness of the short line and the well-observed
enjambment. The poems appear to love movement backwards,
behind, and inwards as in the opening short poem:

Behind the word there is a shadow
Behind the shadow a farm with house and trees
Behind the trees a bright, green field
Thought cannot reach

('Behind the Word there is a Shadow')

Vaage's rooms are self-sufficient and have porous walls that
welcome loss easily. Each line acts as a glacial layer, transparently
adding weight to the whole:

You do not need to build
anything for me
I built these rooms myself
from nails and snow
I would rather you shut out the day
Took rooms away
                    ('You Do Not Need To Build')

Alongside shorter lyrics is a lengthy sequence that follows the internal and external unfolding of the life of a sheep farmer in the wilds of Norway. This reclusive figure never outstays his welcome:

Ask for the farmer
he is invisible
He is gone just like his animals
They are inside the half-darkened
cold room
Where is the farmer?
His traces are in the snow
His boots
are clean as air
                    ('The Sheep Farmer')

The later poems 'From the Institution' are just as hauntingly simple. Vaage continues to build corridors of self-contained rooms within a sequence of fifteen prose poems:

The car charged the roof and walls in the old house with energy. It sprayed an innocent foam into the empty spaces so I could settle down. But the peace the car gave me was only temporary. I could stand stillness for a while because the car promised motion. Small bubbles emerged from the wires long after I parked.
                    ('The Car Ride')

One of the recurring enigmatic figures from *Outside the Institution* is the absent father. The translators Hanne Bramness and Frances Presley capture the parental relationship precisely with the minimized use of punctuation, most notably full stops; the effect collaborates with the line break to invite the silence in. The unpunctuated images of the father float upwards after each reading and relocate elsewhere reinforcing the father's standing in other poems from across the selected collection. The subject of the poem is connected and yet removed, this sense of closeness and otherness is what makes Vaage's poetic process compelling:

> My father has gone to the other side of the valley
> He calls from the old phone booth by the village road
> The red metal booth no one uses any more
> The phone in the booth still works
> Blind, my father searches for change in his pockets
> He drops coins down through the bars of the floor
> My father searches for coins with
> His thin fingers with nails that are too long
>
> ('My Father Has Gone')

Charismatic, with a strong dose of humility are the defining qualities of András Mezei's poetry in *Christmas in Auschwitz*. In his valuable introduction Thomas Ország-Land recreates the blueprint behind the poems, navigating through Mezei's own survival of the holocaust and their meeting and recovery in the Hungarian Holocaust camp for Jewish children, to the translating of Mezei's Holocaust poetry towards the end of his life. A literary journalist most of his career, Mezei made a substantial contribution to Hungary's cultural and social development: 'Like many Holocaust survivors of his generation he embraced enthusiastically the ideal of Communism in the hope of building a just society free of racial, religious and class prejudice.'

On first handling, *Christmas in Auschwitz* appears to be a slim volume, yet within its pages is a deep cavern containing fifty-one poems. The verses form crevices in an echo chamber where the

language is deceptively still. Mezei's poems are starkly convincing
in their imagery and moral stance and operate with such a light
touch and yet the backdrop of suffering is always present and in
conversation with the poet's tone.

> . . . She stands outside by the well-wrung mop
> that she has placed before her threshold,
> she goes on rinsing the long red passageway
> to welcome a new arrival.
> She will never leave the ghetto
> Not till her younger son returns
> . . . although she knows he will not.
>
> ('Blanche Schwarcz')

Mezei's genteel tone is in keeping with the piece-making
approach of these poems. The poems were cut from a tattered
cloth of collected facts, records, correspondences, interviews,
post-war criminal proceedings, and personal experiences. Mezei
handles each fragment with such spareness and measures images
against an exacting rhythm. The finished poems are unrelenting
acts of remembrance. The lines reverberate alongside deafening
silences, and deafening heartbeats:

> It doesn't matter which wagon it was, and
> whose lips held fast against the crack
> between the planks of the cattle truck,
> who sucked clean air through that tiny space,
> which district filled his lungs with the fragrance
> of rain-soaked hay, of snow on the meadows
> it no longer matters who found that teat,
> in that crowded box-car amidst the putrid
> steam of urine and stench of excrement,
> who found it crawling among sore feet,
> that nipple bursting through the crack
> to feed him on oxygen-enriched air,
> who feasted like a babe on the breast,

which prisoner's life was thus extended,
whether it was a Jew or a Serbian
whether a Russian or a Hungarian
whose heart at last could beat more calmly,
who has gained strength whilst surrounded by death –

and whose eyes have locked on to an unearthly crack
ever since then, in this blinded wagon
which is our world, that crack, that crack
admitting a light beyond our reality,
a light through which the whole train of cattle-trucks
passes forever with all the prisoners –
a light that burns like a beam from hell.

('Cattle Trucks')

With many of the Hungarian Holocaust poets largely ignored in their own towns and with the absence of a comprehensive anthology of Hungarian Holocaust poetry, there is a real danger of the local populations being desensitized and misinformed about the experiences of the survivors and of the legacy of the victims of the Holocaust. Ország-Land's translations are an urgent contribution to the painstakingly gathered histories that continue to erode with each coming generation, who without just cause unwittingly fail to re-ignite, to re-imagine the hidden, and the disavowed poetries from our most hellish times.

See *MPT* 3/8 for more poems by Tsvetanka Elenkova and MPT 3/13 for more from *Christmas in Auschwitz.*

*Saradha Soobrayen*

(Correction: Please note MPT3/13 'Transplants', page 232, last two lines, the quotation should read: 'It was the little tongue that struck me most/ in mum's last hours, tiny like a bird's'.)

# Notes on Contributors

**Timothy Allen** was teaching at the National University of the Peruvian Amazon in the early 1990s when he first heard the music of Chabuca Granda and discovered the poetry of Javier Heraud. He recently completed a reworking of Vietnam's national epic, *Kiều*, and in May 2010 joined the advisory board of *Sea Breeze*, the Journal of Contemporary Liberian Writings (www.liberiaseabreeze.com).

**Shon Arieh-Lerer's** poems, translations, and reviews have appeared in magazines such as *Circumference, Beloit Poetry Journal, Chronogram*, and *World Literature Today*. His poem 'Chickasaw Silence' received a 2008 Our American Indian Heritage Award citation. He lives in Brooklyn, New York.

**Tony Baker**, born 1954 in South London, studied piano and composition at Trinity College of Music, London, and literature in Cambridge and Durham. He has worked variously as an ecologist, *répétiteur*, dustman, youth hostel warden. Editor of the magazine FIGS in the '80s, his own writing has appeared in journals and books (most recently *In Transit*, Reality Street, 2005) over the last 30 years. He lives and works as a musician in France.

**Richard Berengarten** (formerly Burns) is author of many books of poetry, most recently the first five volumes of his *Selected Writings* (Salt, 2008). *The Salt Companion to Richard Berengarten* is due out autumn 2010. His poetry has been translated into more than 90 languages and he has received many prizes. He founded the international Cambridge Poetry Festival.

**Charles Cantalupo's** recent work includes *War and Peace in Contemporary Eritrean Poetry* (2009), *Who Needs a Story? Contemporary Eritrean Poetry in Tigrinya, Tigre and Arabic* (2006), and a documentary – *Against All Odds: African Languages and Literatures into the 21st Century* (2007). He is Distinguished Professor of English, Comparative Literature, and African Studies at Penn State University.

Punjabi poet and essayist **Amarjit Chandan** has published two collections in English translation *Sonata for Four Hands* (Arc 2010) and *Being Here* (The Many Press, 1993, 1995, 2005). His work has appeared in many magazines including *Modern Poetry in Translation*. He was amongst ten British poets on Radio 3 selected by Andrew Motion on National Poetry Day in 2001.

**Murray Citron** spoke Yiddish as a child. He came recently on the poetry of Itzik Manger and is recovering his Yiddish to read the poems. He has high school German and is grateful for the prose translations by Peter Branscombe in the Penguin Heine.

**Alfred Corn** has published nine books of poetry, a novel, and two collections of essays in the USA. He took a graduate degree in French literature at Columbia University and has translated from French, German, Spanish, Italian, Portuguese, and classical Greek. He spends half of every year in England.

**Sasha Dugdale's** third collection of poetry *The Red House* will be published by Carcanet Oxford Poets in 2011.

**Vivian Eden** was born in the United States and lives in Jerusalem. She holds a Ph.D. in translation studies from the University of Iowa and works for the newspaper *Haaretz English Edition / The International Herald Tribune*. *Front and Back*, her poems in English with translations into Hebrew by various hands, came out in 2008 in the Kvar Series at Carmel Publishing.

**John Greening** received a Cholmondeley Award in 2008. He was this year made a Hawthornden Fellow and a Fellow of the English Association. He has published studies of the Poets of the First World War, Yeats, Hardy, Edward Thomas and Elizabethan Love Poets. His *Hunts: Poems 1979-2009* includes several poems on Akhenaten.

**Dorothea Grünzweig,** born in Korntal, Germany, has lived in Finland since 1989 as a teacher, freelance writer and translator. Her many publications include four award-winning collections of poetry, all with Wallstein Verlag, most recently *Glasstimmen lasinäänet*, 2004, and *Die Auflösung, 2008*.

**Nicky Harman** lives in the UK. She works as a literary translator as well as teaching on a translation studies course at Imperial College London. She is currently working on the novel *Gold Mountain Blues*, by Zhang Ling, and a volume of Han Dong's poetry.

**Robert Hull** has published four books of poetry, the most recent being *On Portsmouth Station* (Beafred, 2008). His titles for children include history, poetry anthologies, and retellings of myth. He has written two books about teaching: *Behind the Poem* (Routledge 1988); and *The Language Gap* (Methuen), a critical account of language practices in schooling.

**John Irons**, born 1942, studied French, German and Dutch at Cambridge, where he wrote a Ph. D. thesis on poetic imagery. A professional translator for twenty years, his poetry translations have mainly been from Dutch and the Scandinavian languages. He lives in Odense, Denmark.

**W.D. Jackson** has lived and worked in Italy and, since 1973, in Munich. The first two books of his work-in-progress, *Then and Now – Words in the Dark* (2002) and *From Now to Then* (2005) are published by Menard Press. *Boccaccio in Florence and Other Poems* came out in 2009 from Shearsman / Menard.

**Naomi Jaffa** was born in 1961, grew up in London and North Yorkshire and read English at Oxford. She is Director of The Poetry Trust, the organisation behind Aldeburgh Poetry Festival for which she has worked since 1993. She has published one short collection, *The Last Hour of Sleep* (Five Leaves Press, 2003).

**Emily Jeremiah** lectures in German at Royal Holloway. She is the author of *Troubling Maternity*, and of fiction, articles and reviews. In 2008, she was awarded joint third prize in *The Times* Stephen Spender poetry translation competition. Her translations of poems by Eeva-Liisa Manner were published by Waterloo Press as *Bright, Dusky, Bright* in 2009. She lives in London.

**Steve Komarnyckyj** is a British Ukrainian writer whose literary translations and poems have appeared in a range of magazines. He has been interviewed on Ukrainian television and by the *Den* (Day) newspaper and the influential Ukrainian weekly *Dzerkalo Tyzhnya* and his Ukrainian language articles have appeared in *2000*, a Kyiv newspaper, and on the Unian website.

**Paschalis Nikolaou** received his Ph.D. from the University of East Anglia, and currently teaches literary translation at the Ionian University (Corfu). Reviews, essays, translations and poems have appeared in English and Greek journals. He has co-edited *Translating Selves: Experience and Identity between Languages and Literatures* (Continuum, 2008), and is reviews editor of the translation journal *mTm*.

**Dasha C. Nisula** teaches and translates Slavic literature. She has published two books of poetry in translation. Her translations have appeared in the *Pennsylvania Review, Colorado Review, IQ: International Quarterly, MPT* and, most recently, *The Dirty Goat* and *Absinthe: New European Writing*. She works at Western Michigan University.

**Padraig Rooney's** *In The Bonsai Garden* won the Patrick Kavanagh Award in 1986. His second collection *The Escape Artist* (Smith/Doorstop) won The Poetry Business competition in 2006. *The Fever Wards* has just been published by Salt in October. He lives in Basel, Switzerland.

**Cecilia Rossi** holds an MA in Creative Writing from Cardiff University and a Ph.D. in Literary Translation from the University of East Anglia. Her translations of the *Selected Poems of Alejandra Pizarnik* are forthcoming with Waterloo Press (autumn 2010).

**Anthony Rudolf** has contributed translations to *MPT* quite regularly over the last forty years, mainly from French and Russian. His latest book is a collection of prose and verse sequences, *Zigzag* (Carcanet and Northern House).

**Adam J. Sorkin's** books of translation include *Memory Glyphs: Three Prose Poets from Romania* (Twisted Spoon, 2009), Mircea Ivănescu's *lines poems poetry* (University of Plymouth, 2009), and Carmen Firan's *Rock and Dew* (Sheep Meadow, 2010). Sorkin is Distinguished Professor of English, Penn State Brandywine.

**Anne Stevenson**, for the past fifty years an Anglo-American dual-national, is the author of over twenty books of poetry and criticism. Her collected *Poems 1955–2005* (Bloodaxe) won the Lannan Lifetime Achievement Award. Her latest collection, *Stone Milk* (also Bloodaxe) appeared in 2008.

**Saradha Soobrayen** is the Poetry Editor of *Chroma*: A LGBT Literary Arts Journal. Her poetry appears in the *Red Anthology* 2009, *The Forward Anthology* 2008, and *Oxford Poets Anthology* 2007. She received an Eric Gregory Award in 2004.

**D.M.Thomas** has won a Cholmondeley award for poetry and the Orwell Prize for his biography of Solzhenitsyn. His novel *The White Hotel* has been translated into thirty languages. His translations of Pushkin and Akhmatova have been widely praised. His most recent verse collection is *Flight and Smoke* (Francis Boutle). www.dmthomasonline.net

**Stefan Tobler's** translation of Roger Willemsen's *An Afghan Journey*, won English PEN's Writers in Translation prize. His translations of Antônio Moura will appear in Arc's Visible Poets series. He has published poems and translations in journals such as *Shearsman* and *MPT* . He is setting up And Other Stories, a not-for-private-profit organization to publish international fiction (www.andotherstories. org).

**Damian Walford Davies** teaches in the Department of English and Creative Writing at Aberystwyth University. His collection *Suit of Lights* (A Welsh Literature Exchange 'Bookshelf' Choice) appeared in 2009; he is currentlycompleting a collection entitled *Alabaster Girls*.

**Stephen Watts** is a poet, editor and translator. His most recent work is *Mountain Language/Lingua di montagna* (Hearing Eye 2009). He edited the Punjabi poet Amarjit Chandan's *Sonata For Four Hands* and co-translated Meta Kušar's *Ljubljana* (both from Arc Publications 2010). He is also co-translating, with Cristina Viti, a short novel by Reza Baraheni.

**Judith Wilkinson** is a British poet and translator. She grew up in the Netherlands and is fully bilingual. Her translation of Toon Tellegen's *About Love and About Nothing Else* was published by Shoestring Press in 2008. Carcanet will publish her translation of his *Raptors* in February 2011.

**Karen McCarthy Woolf** was born in London to English and Jamaican parents. Her poetry has been exhibited on London Underground, broadcast on BBC radio and is anthologised in *Ten: New Poets from Spread the Word* (Bloodaxe).

**Derk Wynand,** born in Bad Suderode, Germany, has lived in Canada since 1952. He has published several works translated from the German of H.C. Artmann, Erich Wolfgang Skwara and Dorothea Grünzweig. His eleventh collection of poems, *Past Imperfect, Present Tense,* is scheduled for publication this fall by Bayeux Arts.

# FREED SPEECH

### Edited by David and Helen Constantine

Cover by Lucy Wilkinson

## Contents

Price £9.95
   Available from www.mptmagazine.com

MODERN POETRY IN TRANSLATION   Series 3   Number 13

*TRANSPLANTS*

Edited by David and Helen Constantine

Cover by Lucy Wilkinson

**Contents**

Gregory Warren Wilson, 'Himalayan Poppy'
András Mezei, five poems from *Christmas in Auschwitz*, translated by Thomas Ország-Land
Itzik Manger, four poems, translated by Murray Citron
Amir Or, 'The City', translated by Pascale Petit and the author
Norbert Hirschhorn, 'My Cousin the Greenhorn'
Tahar Bekri, 'Epic of the thyme of Palestine', translated by Marilyn Hacker
Sappho, 'Fragment 96', translated by Will Heath
Roger Moulson, six poems from *The Greek Anthology*
Horace III, 30, translated by Paul Harris
Du Fu, three poems, translated by Jonathan Waley
Miklós Radnóti, four poems, translated by Stephen Capus
Four Afghan Poems, translated from the Persian by Zuzanna Olszewska
Amina Saïd, two poems, translated by Marilyn Hacker
Alejandra Pizarnik, poems, translated by Cecilia Rossi
Kristiina Ehin, seven poems, translated by Ilmar Lehtpere
Francis Combes, four poems, translated by Alan Dent
Blanca Varela, four poems, translated by Ruth Fainlight
Amelia Rosselli, extracts from *Variazioni belliche*, translated by Cristina Viti
Brecht, ten poems, translated by David Constantine

Reviews
Rowyda Amin on Marilyn Hacker's Vénus Khoury-Ghata
Meryl Pugh on two anthologies of African poetry
Eric Ormsby on an anthology of modern Italian poetry and Anamaria Crowe Serrano' Annamarie Ferramosca
Roger Moulson on Yang Lian
Saradha Soobrayen: Further Reviews

Price £9.95
   Available from www.mptmagazine.com

# *MPT* Subscription Form

| Name | Address |
|------|---------|
| Phone | Postcode |
| E-mail | Country |

I would like to subscribe to *Modern Poetry in Translation* (please tick relevant box):

**Subscription Rates** (including postage by surface mail)

|  | UK | Overseas |
|---|---|---|
| ❑ One year subscription (2 issues) | £19.90 | £25 / US$ 38 |
| ❑ Two year subscription (4 issues) with discount | £36 | £46 / US$ 69 |

Student Discount*

|  | | |
|---|---|---|
| ❑ One year subscription (2 issues) | £16 | £21 / US$ 32 |
| ❑ Two year subscription (4 issues) | £28 | £38 / US$ 57 |

Please indicate which year you expect to complete your studies 20 . . .

Standing Order Discount (only available to UK subscribers)

| | |
|---|---|
| ❑ Annual subscription (2 issues) | £18 |
| ❑ Student rate for annual subscription (2 issues)* | £14 |

**Payment Method** (please tick appropriate box)

❑ **Cheque:** please make cheques payable to: *Modern Poetry in Translation*.
Sterling, US Dollar and Euro cheques accepted.

❑ **Standing Order:** please complete the standing order request below, indicating the date you would like your first payment to be taken. This should be at least one month after you return this form. We will set this up directly with your bank. Subsequent annual payments will be taken on the same date each year. For UK only.

| | |
|---|---|
| Bank Name | Account Name |
| Branch Address | ❑ Please notify my bank |
| | Please take my first payment on |
| Post Code | ......./......./......... and future payments on |
| Sort Code | the same date each year. |
| Account Number | Signature: |
| | Date........./........./............ |

**Bank Use Only:** In favour of Modern Poetry in Translation, Lloyds TSB, 1 High St, Carfax, Oxford, OX1 4AA, UK a/c 03115155 Sort-code 30-96-35

Please return this form to: The Administrator, Modern Poetry in Translation, The Queen's College, Oxford, OX1 4AW   administrator@mptmagazine/www.mptmagazine.com